Come into the Light

Nov 2020
To Jessica
and Will

with

warm regards

Tony

Come into the Light

TONY SCULLY

RESOURCE *Publications* · Eugene, Oregon

COME INTO THE LIGHT

For the gospel texts, I chose The American Standard Version (ASV) for its language and its remarkable history. The ASV is in universal public domain.

The ASV is rooted in the Revised Version (RV), a 19th-century British revision of the King James Version of 1611. In 1870, an invitation was extended to American religious leaders for scholars to work on the RV project. A year later, Protestant theologian Philip Schaff chose 30 scholars representing the denominations of Baptist, Congregationalist, Dutch Reformed, Friends, Methodist, Episcopal, Presbyterian, Protestant Episcopal, and Unitarian. The ASV is the basis of the Revised Standard Version, 1971, the Amplified Bible, 1965, the New American Standard Bible, 1995, and the Recovery Version, 1999. A fifth revision, known as the World English Bible, was published in 2000 and was placed in the public domain.

The earlier title of *Come into the Light, Jesus Redux,* by Anthony Patrick Scully is registered with the Library of Congress. Registration Number:

Resource Publications
An Imprint of Wipf and Stock Publishers
199 W. 8th Ave., Suite 3
Eugene, OR 97401

www.wipfandstock.com

PAPERBACK ISBN: 978-1-7252-7997-1
HARDCOVER ISBN: 978-1-7252-7996-4
EBOOK ISBN: 978-1-7252-7998-8

Manufactured in the U.S.A.   08/19/20

In memory of

CHIP SUMMERS
1945–2020

You shine within us, outside us—even darkness shines—when we remember

—THE LORD'S PRAYER, TRANSLATED FROM THE ARAMAIC

Contents

Preface

Come into the Light offers an outspoken conversation with the gospels, four accounts of the life of Jesus of Nazareth. Written by the evangelists, Matthew, Mark, Luke, and John at different times for different audiences, the gospels confront us with arguably the most transformative teaching in our known history. The wisdom of the great masters among us: Jesus; the Buddha; Mohammed, speak of universal compassion, love, and forgiveness. Jesus pointedly preaches that one will find God, not in beseeching what amounts to an anthropomorphic idol, but in searching one's own heart, as in his fundamental teaching, "the kingdom of God is within you" (Luke 17:21). Tony Scully's poems in *Come into the Light* address the central figure of the gospels with questioning, irreverence, and occasional confrontation; in his view many of the stories, even that of the Resurrection itself, seem to hinge on miracles, reflecting earlier religions, both pagan and pre-Christian, that expected gods to cure illnesses, raise the dead, and even to walk on water, rather than on the powers of compassion, love, and forgiveness that characterize Jesus.

As in his earlier book, *A Carolina Psalter (Wipf & Stock, 2019)*, Scully asserts the authority of the individual voice in our search for a God beyond accepted boundaries and definitions. Here, he affirms Jesus as a living presence of compassion within the open heart. I

Is Jesus divine? Is that really the message? Or the point? Scully suggests that when Christian tradition moved away from the indwelling presence of Jesus in our hearts and began to pray to him to bless wars and deliver us from sickness and death, they robbed him of his transformational power, the very reason he walked among us. In effect, to worship him is to destroy him.

Why these gospel stories and not others? What structure guides the narrative? The explanation is evident: The familiar story of Jesus as a man who is born, grows up, begins a public ministry, is executed by the state, and who rises from the dead, begins and ends with light. In the over 100 passages in *Come into the Light*, Jesus manifests uncommon wisdom; as he moves forward in his mission, he brings abundance, healing, and new interpretations of human behavior, especially in the Beatitudes. Where the stories emphasize miracles as proof of divinity, the poems question whether, in fact, Jesus offers a deeper understanding of why he lives among us. What guides the narrative is ongoing conversation and questioning about the nature of Jesus. In the author's view, the heart of Jesus is proof enough of his transcendence. *Come into the Light* is the second book of poems in a trilogy addressing foundation texts.

Acknowledgments

Thank you to the following people for their assistance with the publication of *Come into the Light:* to my wife, Joy Claussen Scully for her constant support and love over thirty-five years; to Richard Brown, Director of the University of South Carolina Press, who with his typical generosity put me in touch with Wipf & Stock; to the late Reverend Dr. William F. ("Chip") Summers for his infinite wisdom, his unfailing sense of humor in all matters secular and profane, and for his kindness to struggling poets; to Marty Daniels, a light-keeper, for her unerring eye and typical good judgment; to Earl Bryant, MD for his sense of reality and ironic wit after a lifetime of practicing medicine; to Drew Casper, PhD, University of Southern California School of Cinematic Arts, a close friend since we were teenagers, for his enthusiasm for my work, even for my worst instincts; to Nina von Eckardt, artist and critic extraordinaire, for her bright spirit that never fails; to Ponza and Robert Vaughan, the best of friends and readers; to Kate Mullikin and Daniel Sheldon for their love of art and song and me; and to Herb Martin for his decades of being there.

Introduction

In 325 the Council of Nicaea, following some earlier views, decreed that Jesus of Nazareth, the humble rabbi who preached unconditional love and forgiveness as a way of life, was now to be addressed as the Second Person of the Blessed Trinity, on a par with God the Father and God the Holy Ghost, or Holy Spirit. In other words, Jesus of Nazareth was now God. Over the centuries, as this doctrine took hold, often at the risk of losing one's head, one had to believe in the divinity of Jesus if one was to call oneself a Christian.

For those who believe in Spirit, death has traditionally been understood as the threshold of a deeper reality. To believers, the souls of the dead, certainly those of Jesus, Mary, and Joseph, remain as alive as everyone else who has passed into that dimension we call the afterlife, in all fairness to the argument a domain that remains little understood or accessible.

With *Come into the Light*, I felt it was time to speak. The gospels of Matthew, Mark, Luke, and John, as with the Psalms, have been with us in the Judeo-Christian tradition in every worship service, every prayer meeting, and every Mass for generation upon generation, their compelling teachings evident. As we become increasingly fixated on nuclear weapons and armaments, however, we cannot avoid inevitable questions: If our indwelling deity, Jesus Christ, is truly the Prince of Peace, why are we constantly at war? Even as we pray in good faith, is "Jesus" a euphemism for Thor, the Nordic war god associated with thunder and lightning? If Jesus is our Lord and Master as the gospels maintain, why are so many of the best of us addicted to fighting? Why so much gun violence? Why so much addiction? Why so many suicides? Who is this Jesus?

The pervasive kindness of believers in small towns and cities across the American South suggests they are deeply touched by the Bible, especially by the Jesus of the gospels. From prayers to "Our Lord and Savior," come armies of compassionate, world-serving people who in the imitation of Christ serve the homeless, the hungry, the grieving, and the incarcerated with warm hearts and the best of intentions. For many others, however, the Bible sets forth outmoded or impossible absolutes, notably the injunctions about the place of women and slaves. The New Testament teaching that Jesus is divine, and that he died for our sins, however potent a touchstone for argument, yea or nay, does not necessarily placate the wounded heart.

The real question is about the nature of God. In this particular context, how is Jesus God? Many of the most progressive minds on the planet hardly believe in Spirit at all. Others argue for God as Mind or Creative Source. How is Jesus of Nazareth Creative Source? Whole theologies, perhaps not intentionally, describe a spiritual universe predicated on good versus evil: the forces of light versus the forces of darkness. These interpretations run deep in our DNA and show up in our prayers and in our Scripture. In many cases, this duality underpins and reinforces well-intentioned theological thinking — feeding into national and international conflicts and unrest, as in "God is on our side," or in this case, "Jesus will heal. Jesus will protect us." Many violent and repressive regimes shared the same beliefs, unfortunately.

We Americans are increasingly a nation at war. Extended wars. We are four percent of the world's population; we spend more money on defense than the next ten countries combined. Are we creating yet another empire? Where are we going?

As a young man, I became a Jesuit when I joined the Society of Jesus, a choice that set me on an almost unending spiritual quest. The Jesuits, then as now, were committed to social justice and to scholarship, which is not to say every denomination, religious order, congregation, and sect does not embrace its own philosophies about what galvanized its founders; namely, the worship of God as they understood God. The Calvinists, as one example, following their understanding of God, are passionate about building a better and more equitable Earth. We are not so different.

The advancing conservatism in the Catholic Church in the seventies and eighties effectively closed down open-minded theological scholarship and discussion in American Catholic colleges and universities. During that period, when an almost ferocious evangelical movement seemed determined to influence local and national politics, the question, "Who is God?" sounded almost heretical. Believers knew for sure who God was. If the Bible didn't tell them so, they knew absolutely that the Holy Spirit was the guiding presence in the Christian church and family. Even the most hidebound understood the commonality of the different Christian communities and were beginning to open themselves to the idea that non-Christians were worshipping the same God.

For some of us, self-professed spiritualists in an emerging culture of non-belief, especially in Manhattan, where I lived for many years, it seemed a truism that if the Bible was revealed truth, so were Mozart and Bach, Beethoven, Georgia O'Keeffe, and Shakespeare, not to mention Einstein, Marie Curie, Nikola Tesla, and Thomas Edison, and about a million other creative people who somehow channeled new visions and new understanding of the universe, continually unlocking what had been called "the secrets" in physics, chemistry, and biology. Talk to any composer: he or she might tell you they serve as vehicles for energies that pour through them, from where they are never sure. I remember a literary agent many years ago, possibly in flight from orthodoxy, who ridiculed that idea outright: "Channeling — what a fanciful superstition"! But she wasn't a composer, was she?

In the early seventies, still a Jesuit, after my three years at the Yale School of Drama, where I also served as a deacon for the Reverend William Sloane Coffin Jr., as well as being Writer in Residence at Joseph Papp's Public Theatre one year after graduation, I worked for five years as Project Director of the Jesuit-sponsored Woodstock Center for Religion and Worship, no connection to the rock festival, at the Interchurch Center, 475 Riverside Drive, New York. Its mission: the exploration and renewal of liturgy in collaboration with such leading anthropologists, sociologists, psychologists, and theologians as Rollo May and Jungian Edward C. Whitmont. Dr. Whitmont, a former colleague of Carl Jung, spoke about the revelation of personal and collective truth in dreams and trance states. He had also observed his patients in group therapy dreaming the same dreams. He spoke of patients reexperiencing trauma from past lives. In short, the language of belief was expanding before us. During that time, I also wrote a series of Prayers of the Faithful for Benziger Brothers, a liturgical press that offered contemporary language to the Prayers of the Faithful for the Youth Mass, as it was called. The prayers invoked everyone from John Lennon to Billie Holiday and Nelson Mandela. The idea was to stimulate like-minded language and thinking — to open up windows and doors to the world, especially the world of creativity, often in a surrounding landscape of suffering and violence. My thinking even then, aligned with Martin Luther's idea that all believers were priests.

Once again, the question loomed: Who decides what voices come from God? Who draws the line between the secular and the profane? One might as well ask who has the authority to recognize love. Are we so blinded by the horrors of the twentieth century we cannot see the light in the darkness?

By the time I left the Society of Jesus after fourteen years in 1973, a prominent theologian made the public comment that what believers shared in common were not doctrinal certainties or any clear definition of God, but that in an age of increasing non-belief we were asking the eternal questions — and the questions said it all: "Who is God? Who are we in relation to God? What happens when we die"? The operative point: how could any belief system pin down God? You'd have to be arrogant or stupid to think so.

In the beginning of my new life outside the institutional Church, I chose not to be ordained a priest. The gulf between my personal beliefs and the official teaching had grown too wide. Since then, after a lifetime of questioning, I embrace all religions with love and reverence and take orders from none.

Today, my wife, Joy, and I live in South Carolina. As mayor of a small city here I spent many hours in many churches, especially at funerals and anniversary services, praising the name of God. The South is a culture of hymns and blessings. As we press forward with our exuberant spirits in this extraordinary place, we also live with ghosts. If we listen carefully, we can hear the shouts and cries from the Indian wars, the American Revolution, the Civil War, and feel the sorrows of the enslaved.

My journey into the mysteries of spiritual awareness has been a long one and continues to open into the future. I wrote *Come into the Light* for people who are searching, as I am, for a God who cannot be reduced to an anthropological identity, a God, if you will, beyond gods, a God almost beyond understanding –– beyond ritual and inherited prayer, a God of a trillion stars and planets, who we have been told by his prophets lives in our simple hearts as the God of love. Let us hope.

Come into the Light—but one voice. Read the gospels. Read the poems. Then, speak in your own voice. Share what comes to you. We will listen.

HIS ONLY BEGOTTEN SON

John 3:16–21

16 For God so loved the world, that he gave his only begotten Son, that whosoever believeth on him should not perish, but have eternal life. 17 For God sent not the Son into the world to judge the world; but that the world should be saved through him. 18 He that believeth on him is not judged: he that believeth not hath been judged already, because he hath not believed on the name of the only begotten Son of God. 19 And this is the judgment, that the light is come into the world, and men loved the darkness rather than the light; for their works were evil. 20 For every one that doeth evil hateth the light, and cometh not to the light, lest his works should be reproved. 21 But he that doeth the truth cometh to the light, that his works may be made manifest, that they have been wrought in God.

Come into the light
Come quick
Before the night invades your soul

Come with your sorrows
And your faults
Indelible and dumb

Come with memories
Of quarrels
Outbursts with idiots
Wounds you have inflicted
On the halt
The autistic

The uninformed

Come with tribal affinities
That smother your heart
And clog your brain

Trip if you will
Over your toes
Bang your head
Break your teeth
As you fall
Headlong into fear

Come anyway

You will see the colors of the light

And a voice will tell you
When all things are known
And everything exposed

And yes

You will be born again

IN THE BEGINNING

John 1:1–11

¹ In the beginning was the Word, and the Word was with God, and the Word was God. ² The same was in the beginning with God. ³ All things were made through him; and without him was not anything made that hath been made. ⁴ In him was life; and the life was the light of men. ⁵ And the light shineth in the darkness; and the darkness apprehended it not. ⁶ There came a man, sent from God, whose name was John. ⁷ The same came for witness, that he might bear witness of the light, that all might believe through him. ⁸ He was not the light, but came that he might bear witness of the light. ⁹ There was the true light, even the light which lighteth every man, coming into the world. ¹⁰ He was in the world, and the world was made through him, and the world knew him not. ¹¹ He came unto his own, and they that were his own received him not.

In the beginning was the Word
And the Word was with God
And the Word was God

Who said?

Where was the explosion
And the bang?

In the beginning was Mind
And so-called Sensibility

Unless you otherwise believe

Some wage war
Over terms and preconditions
Asserting there is no cause
Except grenades
No meaning
Only happenstance

Who decided Word?

To think
We may be conceived
Out of nothing at all
En route
To an abyss

Except
Of course
For the force
Of everything alive

The voice of wind
And thunder
The cry of earth
Insisting on life
The majesty of music
Booming kettledrums
Trumpets blaring

And violins

Afterwards
When all is still
And the mind quiets down
We will know
We are possessed

By madness

And the intent
To love

THE WORD WAS MADE FLESH

John 1:12–14

The Word was made flesh
In him was life
And the life was the light of men

For two thousand years
At the latest reckoning
We are told
The light is shining bright
Yes, Ma'am

We remember God is love
Relentlessly

At all costs
We continue on
Arsenals our higher power
Survival our indwelling deity

In this planetary scheme
Orgasm is ecstasy

Why not?

Money
Coin
Portfolios
Deliver meaning
And resolve

As for
Turn the other cheek
And love your enemies
That's something to aspire to
When we remember who we are

Write that down

In the meantime
As it was in the beginning
Is now

And ever shall be

We are warriors

Soldiers to the end

GABRIEL

Luke 1:5–25

⁵ *There was in the days of Herod, king of Judæa, a certain priest named Zacharias, of the course of Abijah: and he had a wife of the daughters of Aaron, and her name was Elisabeth.* ⁶ *And they were both righteous before God, walking in all the commandments and ordinances of the Lord blameless.* ⁷ *And they had no child, because that Elisabeth was barren, and they both were now well stricken in years.*

⁸ *Now it came to pass, while he executed the priest's office before God in the order of his course,* ⁹ *according to the custom of the priest's office, his lot was to enter into the temple of the Lord and burn incense.* ¹⁰ *And the whole multitude of the people were praying without at the hour of incense.* ¹¹ *And there appeared unto him an angel of the Lord standing on the right side of the altar of incense.* ¹² *And Zacharias was troubled when he saw him, and fear fell upon him.* ¹³ *But the angel said unto him, Fear not, Zacharias: because thy supplication is heard, and thy wife Elisabeth shall bear thee a son, and thou shalt call his name John.* ¹⁴ *And thou shalt have joy and gladness; and many shall rejoice at his birth.* ¹⁵ *For he shall be great in the sight of the Lord, and he shall drink no wine nor strong drink; and he shall be filled with the Holy Spirit, even from his mother's womb.* ¹⁶ *And many of the children of Israel shall he turn unto the Lord their God.* ¹⁷ *And he shall go before his face in the spirit and power of Elijah, to turn the hearts of the fathers to the children, and the disobedient to walk in the wisdom of the just; to make ready for the Lord a people prepared for him.* ¹⁸ *And Zacharias said unto the angel, Whereby shall I know this? for I am an old man, and my wife well stricken in years.* ¹⁹ *And the angel answering said unto him, I am Gabriel, that stand in the presence of God; and I was sent to speak unto thee, and to bring thee these good tidings.* ²⁰ *And behold, thou shalt be silent and*

not able to speak, until the day that these things shall come to pass, because thou believedst not my words, which shall be fulfilled in their season. [21] *And the people were waiting for Zacharias, and they marvelled while he tarried in the temple.* [22] *And when he came out, he could not speak unto them: and they perceived that he had seen a vision in the temple: and he continued making signs unto them, and remained dumb.* [23] *And it came to pass, when the days of his ministration were fulfilled, he departed unto his house.* [24] *And after these days Elisabeth his wife conceived; and she hid herself five months, saying,* [25] *Thus hath the Lord done unto me in the days wherein he looked upon me, to take away my reproach among men.*

An angel
Undoubtedly Gabriel
An almost overwhelming energy
Appeared to Elizabeth
Or was it to Mary?
How about both?

His Semitic attraction
Camouflaging
Compressed fire
And urgency

To announce
Elizabeth in her present age
Would bear a son
To usher in
The wisdom of the just

Mary
By the way
Would birth
The savior of mankind
Just that

We know
What happened
In the end:

My God my God
Why has thou forsaken me?

How come
Nobody
I know
Runs into angels anymore?

How come nobody
Feels the force of light?

Has this story become predictable
And old
Ending with severed heads
And borrowed tombs?

These days
Do we really care?

Once the soul kicks in —

Wait

It will

And angels detonate

Anything is possible

At least love

And understanding
Isn't that enough?

Angels between the lines
They're there
Waiting to announce to you
You are more than anything
You ever dreamed

If you are willing to pay the price
For life
Beauty
And unexpected joy

They will never disappoint

JOSEPH

Matthew 1:18–25

¹⁸ Now the birth of Jesus Christ was on this wise: When his mother Mary had been betrothed to Joseph, before they came together she was found with child of the Holy Spirit. ¹⁹ And Joseph her husband, being a righteous man, and not willing to make her a public example, was minded to put her away privily. ²⁰ But when he thought on these things, behold, an angel of the Lord appeared unto him in a dream, saying, Joseph, thou son of David, fear not to take unto thee Mary thy wife: for that which is conceived in her is of the Holy Spirit. ²¹ And she shall bring forth a son; and thou shalt call his name JESUS; for it is he that shall save his people from their sins. ²² Now all this is come to pass, that it might be fulfilled which was spoken by the Lord through the prophet, saying, ²³ Behold, the virgin shall be with child, and shall bring forth a son, And they shall call his name Immanuel; which is, being interpreted, God with us. ²⁴ And Joseph arose from his sleep, and did as the angel of the Lord commanded him, and took unto him his wife; ²⁵ and knew her not till she had brought forth a son: and he called his name JESUS.

Joseph
Who is this angel
You go on about
Proclaiming your bride
Pregnant by the Holy Ghost?

Virgin births have become
Established news
In your corner of the world

Gods with human faces
Diverting the ordinary rules

That said
Is this an advertising stunt
Promoting
Yet another God?

Your son will save his people from their sins?

There's a line

What sins?
The sins of being put upon
Exploited
Used
Jammed into the bog of history
People soon becoming
Skeletons

The sins of being forgotten
Faceless
Anonymous
Unspecified

These days
Most of us resist the idea of virgin births
We do
That
And extraterrestrials too

No offense

Sometimes
Misunderstanding rules

With unexpected consequence

Joseph
Are you a fool
A fall guy
A buffoon?

Or would that be us?

Joseph
We need to talk

THE BIRTH OF JESUS

Luke 2:1–20

¹ *Now it came to pass in those days, there went out a decree from Cæsar Augustus, that all the world should be enrolled.* ² *This was the first enrolment made when Quirinius was governor of Syria.* ³ *And all went to enroll themselves, everyone to his own city.* ⁴ *And Joseph also went up from Galilee, out of the city of Nazareth, into Judæa, to the city of David, which is called Bethlehem, because he was of the house and family of David;* ⁵ *to enroll himself with Mary, who was betrothed to him, being great with child.* ⁶ *And it came to pass, while they were there, the days were fulfilled that she should be delivered.* ⁷ *And she brought forth her firstborn son; and she wrapped him in swaddling clothes, and laid him in a manger, because there was no room for them in the inn.*

⁸ *And there were shepherds in the same country abiding in the field, and keeping watch by night over their flock.* ⁹ *And an angel of the Lord stood by them, and the glory of the Lord shone round about them: and they were sore afraid.* ¹⁰ *And the angel said unto them, Be not afraid; for behold, I bring you good tidings of great joy which shall be to all the people:* ¹¹ *for there is born to you this day in the city of David a Saviour, who is Christ the Lord.* ¹² *And this is the sign unto you: Ye shall find a babe wrapped in swaddling clothes, and lying in a manger.* ¹³ *And suddenly there was with the angel a multitude of the heavenly host praising God, and saying,*

¹⁴ *Glory to God in the highest, And on earth peace among men in whom he is well pleased.*

¹⁵ *And it came to pass, when the angels went away from them into heaven, the shepherds said one to another, Let us now go even unto Bethlehem, and see this thing that is come to pass, which the Lord hath made known unto us.* ¹⁶ *And they came*

with haste, and found both Mary and Joseph, and the babe ly-
ing in the manger. ¹⁷ And when they saw it, they made known
concerning the saying which was spoken to them about this
child. ¹⁸ And all that heard it wondered at the things which
were spoken unto them by the shepherds. ¹⁹ But Mary kept all
these sayings, pondering them in her heart. ²⁰ And the shep-
herds returned, glorifying and praising God for all the things
that they had heard and seen, even as it was spoken unto them.

Once again angels
Once again birth

360,000 people
Born today
And every day

Why is this one different?
Is not every child a savior?

Shepherds in the field
Suggest the slaughterhouse
Eternal light in fields of shit
Is that it?

Send in the clowns
Magic required

Angels we have heard on high

Divinity reveals itself
In ordinary things
Like you and me
Could that possibly be true?

Virgin birth

Shorthand for creativity
Esoteric symbolism
Escaping sex and earth and blood
And undoubtedly adultery
Is that the best
A god can do?

The rest of us
Live on the street
In the bed
The fields
The factory floor
Working
Begging
Going along to get along
Selling our souls for Subarus
And bread

Our prisons
And our hospitals
Jammed with pain
Our higher power
Opioids

We are the dispossessed
The evicted
The disinherited
Still dreaming of gods we have never met
And do not understand

Robbed of explanation
About who we are
And where we are going

At the mercy of ourselves

What do you expect of us?

Every sect
Holds fantasies of parthenogenesis
Ain't that the case?
Leda and the swan
Osiris
Mithras
Magical mystery tours

Dreams pile up
Bursting with resurrection
And winged chariots
Heading into the stratosphere

It's not over
Wait

Presently
We come again to Angel Gabriels
Exploding into light
Publicizing saviors
Deliverers
Yet more divinities

The message:
Help is coming
The good news has arrived

Would you like to be saved?
Why not?
In that case
Make a wish
Click your heels

Turn 'round three times

And believe, goddamn, believe!

P.S. Lord have mercy
On our complicated

Unbelieving

Contradictory

Souls

THE MAGI

Matthew 2:1–12

¹ *Now when Jesus was born in Bethlehem of Judœa in the days of Herod the king, behold, Wise-men from the east came to Jerusalem, saying,* ² *Where is he that is born King of the Jews? for we saw his star in the east, and are come to worship him.* ³ *And when Herod the king heard it, he was troubled, and all Jerusalem with him.* ⁴ *And gathering together all the chief priests and scribes of the people, he inquired of them where the Christ should be born.* ⁵ *And they said unto him, In Bethlehem of Judœa: for thus it is written through the prophet,*

⁶ *And thou Bethlehem, land of Judah,*
Art in no wise least among the princes of Judah:
For out of thee shall come forth a governor,
Who shall be shepherd of my people Israel.

⁷ *Then Herod privily called the Wise-men, and learned of them exactly what time the star appeared.* ⁸ *And he sent them to Bethlehem, and said, Go and search out exactly concerning the young child; and when ye have found him, bring me word, that I also may come and worship him.* ⁹ *And they, having heard the king, went their way; and lo, the star, which they saw in the east, went before them, till it came and stood over where the young child was.* ¹⁰ *And when they saw the star, they rejoiced with exceeding great joy.* ¹¹ *And they came into the house and saw the young child with Mary his mother; and they fell down and worshipped him; and opening their treasures they offered unto him gifts, gold and frankincense and myrrh.* ¹² *And being warned of God in a dream that they should not return to Herod, they departed into their own country another way.*

From out of the east
The Wise Men come
To worship the infant
Born King of the Jews

Gaspar
Melchior
Balthasar
From the Persian priestly caste
According to the Internet
By reputation
Zoroastrians
And international astrologers

A field day for PhDs in eastern languages
And esoteric creeds
What about the rest of us?

Are we surrendering
The legacy
Of Egypt
India
And Tibet
To buttress a story
Out of sync
Even in the stars?

The fire of creation
The thunder of infinite love
Has arrived in Bethlehem
Obliterating considerations
Of the past
Notwithstanding our own insanity

The Magi saw it all

The Baby Savior
Born King of the Jews
Yes, Ma'am
About to reign over two thousand years
Of suffering
And religious wars

Thank you, Jesus

THE HOLY INNOCENTS

Matthew 2:13–23

¹³ *Now when they were departed, behold, an angel of the Lord appeareth to Joseph in a dream, saying, Arise and take the young child and his mother, and flee into Egypt, and be thou there until I tell thee: for Herod will seek the young child to destroy him.* ¹⁴ *And he arose and took the young child and his mother by night, and departed into Egypt;* ¹⁵ *and was there until the death of Herod: that it might be fulfilled which was spoken by the Lord through the prophet, saying, Out of Egypt did I call my son.*

¹⁶ *Then Herod, when he saw that he was mocked of the Wise-men, was exceeding wroth, and sent forth, and slew all the male children that were in Bethlehem, and in all the borders thereof, from two years old and under, according to the time which he had exactly learned of the Wise-men.* ¹⁷ *Then was fulfilled that which was spoken through Jeremiah the prophet, saying,*

> ¹⁸ *A voice was heard in Ramah,*
> *Weeping and great mourning,*
> *Rachel weeping for her children;*
> *And she would not be comforted, because they are not.*

¹⁹ *But when Herod was dead, behold, an angel of the Lord appeareth in a dream to Joseph in Egypt, saying,* ²⁰ *Arise and take the young child and his mother, and go into the land of Israel: for they are dead that sought the young child's life.* ²¹ *And he arose and took the young child and his mother, and came into the land of Israel.* ²² *But when he heard that Archelaus was reigning over Judæa in the room of his father Herod, he was afraid to go thither; and being warned of God in a dream, he withdrew into the parts of Galilee,* ²³ *and came and dwelt in a city called Nazareth; that it might be fulfilled which was spoken through the prophets, that he should be called a Nazarene.*

As the story goes
And night swallows up the soul
King Herod massacred baby boys near Bethlehem
Imagining one might be the Messiah
And replace him
As King of the Jews

Reminding us
Of pogroms and Holocausts

Slaughter of the Holy Innocents
What to make of that?

Some say the account's apocryphal
Guess what?
Herod is alive and well

Illegal children
Caught on the border
Trapped in cages
Down Mexico way
Rohingya babies in Myanmar
Unnamed
Unknown
Mothers terrified they'll be targeted

Evocations of Auschwitz
Children scratching images on walls
Suns and moons
And faces well-fed
Once upon a time

The sexual slave trade's going strong
Isn't it?

Celebrate
You and I are not sacrificial offerings today
On Aztec pyramids
And Mayan pools
Bethlehem
Newtown
And Columbine

A voice is heard in Ramah
Weeping and great mourning

Mothers refusing to be comforted
Their children are no more

We remain paralyzed
Mute
Our Herods are abounding still
Dictators feasting on
Paranoia
And celebrity

If prophets manage to escape their infancy
They will be murdered later on
For interrupting politics
And damaging the Dow

Evolution
As we well know
Comes dropping slow

Ah so

THE BOY JESUS

Luke 2:41–50

⁴¹ *And his parents went every year to Jerusalem at the feast of the passover.* ⁴² *And when he was twelve years old, they went up after the custom of the feast;* ⁴³ *and when they had fulfilled the days, as they were returning, the boy Jesus tarried behind in Jerusalem; and his parents knew it not;* ⁴⁴ *but supposing him to be in the company, they went a day's journey; and they sought for him among their kinsfolk and acquaintance:* ⁴⁵ *and when they found him not, they returned to Jerusalem, seeking for him.* ⁴⁶ *And it came to pass, after three days they found him in the temple, sitting in the midst of the teachers, both hearing them, and asking them questions:* ⁴⁷ *and all that heard him were amazed at his understanding and his answers.* ⁴⁸ *And when they saw him, they were astonished; and his mother said unto him, Son, why hast thou thus dealt with us? behold, thy father and I sought thee sorrowing.* ⁴⁹ *And he said unto them, How is it that ye sought me? knew ye not that I must be in my Father's house?* ⁵⁰ *And they understood not the saying which he spake unto them.*

The wanderings of youth
Bring forth the wisdom of a twelve-year old
Obvious questions
No adult dare speak

Why temples?
Why priests?
A pair of doves?
Say what?

What are you gentlemen doing here?

Does this arrangement
Reassure us
Ancestral gods
Excuse me, God Almighty
Is guarding us?

Protecting us
For a price

I Am Who Am

Does that not apply
To everyone alive?

Disaster prophesied
This child will certainly advise
Turn the other cheek
Assist the poor
The persecuted
The reviled
The meek

Because of him
His mother is informed
A sword will pierce her soul

Following Q&A
The Holy Family
Sagrada Familia
Returned to Nazareth
And the child grew
Into a sign of contradiction

Which is the mark of wisdom

And the bloodshed to come

THE BAPTIST

Matthew 3:1–12

¹ *And in those days cometh John the Baptist, preaching in the wilderness of Judæa, saying,* ² *Repent ye; for the kingdom of heaven is at hand.* ³ *For this is he that was spoken of through Isaiah the prophet, saying,*

> *The voice of one crying in the wilderness,*
> *Make ye ready the way of the Lord,*
> *Make his paths straight.*

⁴ *Now John himself had his raiment of camel's hair, and a leathern girdle about his loins; and his food was locusts and wild honey.* ⁵ *Then went out unto him Jerusalem, and all Judæa, and all the region round about the Jordan;* ⁶ *and they were baptized of him in the river Jordan, confessing their sins.* ⁷ *But when he saw many of the Pharisees and Sadducees coming to his baptism, he said unto them, Ye offspring of vipers, who warned you to flee from the wrath to come?* ⁸ *Bring forth therefore fruit worthy of repentance:* ⁹ *and think not to say within yourselves, We have Abraham to our father: for I say unto you, that God is able of these stones to raise up children unto Abraham.* ¹⁰ *And even now the axe lieth at the root of the trees: every tree therefore that bringeth not forth good fruit is hewn down, and cast into the fire.* ¹¹ *I indeed baptize you in water unto repentance: but he that cometh after me is mightier than I, whose shoes I am not worthy to bear: he shall baptize you in the Holy Spirit and in fire:* ¹² *whose fan is in his hand, and he will thoroughly cleanse his threshing-floor; and he will gather his wheat into the garner, but the chaff he will burn up with unquenchable fire.*

Dionysius in Galilee
A voice
Shrieking in the wilderness

Prepare ye the way of the Lord

Accusing the priests
A brood of vipers
He cries

Try that today

Shout out
About the coming wrath
Speak in apocalyptic images
Prophesying fire
And doom

Your turn

Who is this Baptist?
Battista Baptistes
A hippie riding wild?
A countercultural beat?

Has anyone observed the man's tattoos:
Repent
In red, white, and royal blue

Mother
In Aramaic
Hebrew
Greek
What about Chinese?

We cannot listen
To hysteria
We cannot hear
What sounds like lunacy

Every day the end of the world
The sky falling
The sun on fire

In the meantime
We are told
The Holy Ghost
Is on his way
Or hers

Where is the quiet smile
The playful breeze
Soft upon our cheek?

Why does faith come thundering
And the promise of God
Pierce the silence of the fields?

Maybe the quiet
Will arrive as prophesized

Maybe if we listen
We will hear
The whispering
Of Christ

THE LAMB OF GOD

John 1:29–36

²⁹ On the morrow he seeth Jesus coming unto him, and saith, Behold, the Lamb of God, that taketh away the sin of the world! ³⁰ This is he of whom I said, After me cometh a man who is become before me: for he was before me. ³¹ And I knew him not; but that he should be made manifest to Israel, for this cause came I baptizing in water. ³² And John bare witness, saying, I have beheld the Spirit descending as a dove out of heaven; and it abode upon him. ³³ And I knew him not: but he that sent me to baptize in water, he said unto me, Upon whomsoever thou shalt see the Spirit descending, and abiding upon him, the same is he that baptizeth in the Holy Spirit. ³⁴ And I have seen, and have borne witness that this is the Son of God.

³⁵ Again on the morrow John was standing, and two of his disciples; ³⁶ and he looked upon Jesus as he walked, and saith, Behold, the Lamb of God!

Behold the Lamb of God
An agricultural conceit
Baa Baa Black Sheep
Have you any wool?

Lamb chops
Forty-nine dollars
A pound and a half
At Costco
What about Dean & DeLuca
Walmart?
Hey!

Metaphors can collapse
With a tearing in culture
And a weakening of resolve
Images can go so far

In the highlands
The meadows come barren
Animals raised for the slaughterhouse
No long roam in pastures green

They live contained in pens
Force fed grain
Nutrition measured in milligrams
Robots behead them now

We no longer taste the fields
Or lick the sky
Our meat has no history

We're poor little lambs
Who have lost our way
Wiffenpoofs in our wandering

The slaughterhouse
The truth of it

In the meantime
The Lamb of God
Has taken away the sins of the world

He thinks

THE BAPTISM OF JESUS

Matthew 3:13–17

Then cometh Jesus from Galilee to the Jordan unto John, to be baptized of him. But John would have hindered him, saying, I have need to be baptized of thee, and comest thou to me? But Jesus answering said unto him, Suffer it now: for thus it becometh us to fulfil all righteousness. Then he suffereth him. And Jesus, when he was baptized, went up straightway from the water: and lo, the heavens were opened unto him, and he saw the Spirit of God descending as a dove, and coming upon him; and lo, a voice out of the heavens, saying, This is my beloved Son, in whom I am well pleased.

Come to the River Jordan
Come watch the poor
The dispossessed
The multitudes of river rats
Waiting to be born again

"Repent"!
the Baptist cries
Trees that do not yield good fruit
Will be axed
And flung into the fire

With salvation
Comes theatre
With redemption
House lights please

Skies will open
God will arrive
As a descending dove
And announce
You are his son
In whom he is well pleased

Stick to the text
Yes Ma'am

There you have it
First time out
Father
Son
And Holy Ghost

In the meantime
Immerse yourself well
In imagining

No telling
What will happen next

THE TEMPTATION IN THE DESERT

Matthew 4:1–11

¹ *Then was Jesus led up of the Spirit into the wilderness to be tempted of the devil.* ² *And when he had fasted forty days and forty nights, he afterward hungered.* ³ *And the tempter came and said unto him, If thou art the Son of God, command that these stones become bread.* ⁴ *But he answered and said, It is written, Man shall not live by bread alone, but by every word that proceedeth out of the mouth of God.* ⁵ *Then the devil taketh him into the holy city; and he set him on the pinnacle of the temple,* ⁶ *and saith unto him, If thou art the Son of God, cast thyself down: for it is written,*

> *He shall give his angels charge concerning thee:*
> *and, On their hands they shall bear thee up,*
> *Lest haply thou dash thy foot against a stone.*

⁷ *Jesus said unto him, Again it is written, Thou shalt not make trial of the Lord thy God.* ⁸ *Again, the devil taketh him unto an exceeding high mountain, and showeth him all the kingdoms of the world, and the glory of them;* ⁹ *and he said unto him, All these things will I give thee, if thou wilt fall down and worship me.* ¹⁰ *Then saith Jesus unto him, Get thee hence, Satan: for it is written, Thou shalt worship the Lord thy God, and him only shalt thou serve.* ¹¹ *Then the devil leaveth him; and behold, angels came and ministered unto him.*

Man shall not live by bread alone
Proclaims the rabbi Yeshua
Apparently out of touch
With bread

What about brioche?
Jewish rye?
English muffins anyone?

Let me laugh
When the world careens
And better minds than mine
Zigzag into night

In a dazzling demonstration
The devil displays
Bahrain
Monte Carlo
Aspen
Malibu
How about the Hassler Roof?

I will give it all to thee
He says
If thou wilt fall down and worship me

But Darlin'
We already do

Who doesn't want an infinity pool
A house on every continent
Hollywood coke
The Rothschilds dropping by?

Be best
Be bad
Proclaims
The inner prostitute

We're still living in North Hollywood

In a double wide
Wired
To want it all

We are genetically engineered
And altogether socialized
Open to every possibility
Of money under the table
And across the board

So where's the Lord thy God?

Come soon
Come loud
Come silently
However you please

Your move

ANGELS ONCE AGAIN

Mark 1:13

[13] And he was in the wilderness forty days tempted of Satan; and he was with the wild beasts; and the angels ministered unto him.

He was with the beasts
And the angels ministered to him

We know about the beasts
Need we enumerate?
Where are the angels?

Once they came in multitudes
Protecting us from road rage
And presidential psychopaths
Singing to celebrate
The interconnected
Overlapping works
Of God and Man
And Rin Tin Tin
Why not?
Why not everything alive?

Where are they now
Why are they invisible?
Have they vanished
Like dinosaurs
And bumblebees?

Were angels at best a peasant fantasy
To make us feel significant?

Imagining
That heaven would appear
And minister
To the likes of us?

Did we really fantasize
They came upon the midnight clear
And stayed throughout the afternoon?

Hark the herald Angels sing
Yes, Ma'am

Hold that thought

UNCLEAN SPIRITS

Mark 1:23-45

²³ *And straightway there was in their synagogue a man with an unclean spirit; and he cried out,* ²⁴ *saying, What have we to do with thee, Jesus thou Nazarene? art thou come to destroy us? I know thee who thou art, the Holy One of God.* ²⁵ *And Jesus rebuked him, saying, Hold thy peace, and come out of him.* ²⁶ *And the unclean spirit, tearing him and crying with a loud voice, came out of him.* ²⁷ *And they were all amazed, insomuch that they questioned among themselves, saying, What is this? a new teaching! with authority he commandeth even the unclean spirits, and they obey him.* ²⁸ *And the report of him went out straightway everywhere into all the region of Galilee round about.*

²⁹ *And straightway, when they were come out of the synagogue, they came into the house of Simon and Andrew, with James and John.* ³⁰ *Now Simon's wife's mother lay sick of a fever; and straightway they tell him of her:* ³¹ *and he came and took her by the hand, and raised her up; and the fever left her, and she ministered unto them.*

³² *And at even, when the sun did set, they brought unto him all that were sick, and them that were possessed with demons.* ³³ *And all the city was gathered together at the door.* ³⁴ *And he healed many that were sick with divers diseases, and cast out many demons; and he suffered not the demons to speak, because they knew him.*

³⁵ *And in the morning, a great while before day, he rose up and went out, and departed into a desert place, and there prayed.* ³⁶ *And Simon and they that were with him followed after him;* ³⁷ *and they found him, and say unto him, All are seeking thee.* ³⁸ *And he saith unto them, Let us go elsewhere into the next towns, that I may preach there also; for to this end*

came I forth. ³⁹ *And he went into their synagogues throughout all Galilee, preaching and casting out demons.*

⁴⁰ *And there cometh to him a leper, beseeching him, and kneeling down to him, and saying unto him, If thou wilt, thou canst make me clean.* ⁴¹ *And being moved with compassion, he stretched forth his hand, and touched him, and saith unto him, I will; be thou made clean.* ⁴² *And straightway the leprosy departed from him, and he was made clean.* ⁴³ *And he strictly charged him, and straightway sent him out,* ⁴⁴ *and saith unto him, See thou say nothing to any man: but go show thyself to the priest, and offer for thy cleansing the things which Moses commanded, for a testimony unto them.* ⁴⁵ *But he went out, and began to publish it much, and to spread abroad the matter, insomuch that Jesus could no more openly enter into a city, but was without in desert places: and they came to him from every quarter.*

Cast out devils now

Unclean energies
You occupy the dark
Where you were born

Your persistent energy
Is war
You cloud the universal mind
With obstinate crusades

Resolving incongruity
With trip wires and booby traps
Wham bam
Thank you, Ma'am

Unrelenting destruction
Invading our dreams
As you intend

What could be more diabolical
Than the declarations of defeat
You plant within our brains
Reminding us
We are nobody
And never were

Once again
We wait for angels
On the horizon
And ask the blessed mothers
To hold us
And keep us safe

Is that so impossible?

THE FIRST MIRACLE

Mark 2:1–12

¹ And when he entered again into Capernaum after some days, it was noised that he was in the house. ² And many were gathered together, so that there was no longer room for them, no, not even about the door: and he spake the word unto them. ³ And they come, bringing unto him a man sick of the palsy, borne of four. ⁴ And when they could not come nigh unto him for the crowd, they uncovered the roof where he was: and when they had broken it up, they let down the bed whereon the sick of the palsy lay. ⁵ And Jesus seeing their faith saith unto the sick of the palsy, Son, thy sins are forgiven. ⁶ But there were certain of the scribes sitting there, and reasoning in their hearts, ⁷ Why doth this man thus speak? he blasphemeth: who can forgive sins but one, even God? ⁸ And straightway Jesus, perceiving in his spirit that they so reasoned within themselves, saith unto them, Why reason ye these things in your hearts? ⁹ Which is easier, to say to the sick of the palsy, Thy sins are forgiven; or to say, Arise, and take up thy bed, and walk? ¹⁰ But that ye may know that the Son of man hath authority on earth to forgive sins (he saith to the sick of the palsy), ¹¹ I say unto thee, Arise, take up thy bed, and go unto thy house. ¹² And he arose, and straightway took up the bed, and went forth before them all; insomuch that they were all amazed, and glorified God, saying, We never saw it on this fashion.

What power lies
Within the heart of us?

We will not know
Until we choose

To own our strength

Take up your bed and walk
He says

Why do we sleep
In middle of wonder?
Why do we drown in noise
Choosing confusion
Over clarity?

We are like puppies
Curling into balls
Not wanting to be recognized
Imagining we will be saved
From unspecified catastrophe
If we make ourselves unknown

Take up your bed and walk

Walk where we say?
Terrified of the unknown destination
And the unfamiliar path

Strange faces
Untried languages
Traditions turned inside out
And upside down

Where is our refuge?

Where is our home?

THE SABBATH

Mark 2:23–28

[23] *And it came to pass, that he was going on the sabbath day through the grainfields; and his disciples began, as they went, to pluck the ears.* [24] *And the Pharisees said unto him, Behold, why do they on the sabbath day that which is not lawful?* [25] *And he said unto them, Did ye never read what David did, when he had need, and was hungry, he, and they that were with him?* [26] *How he entered into the house of God when Abiathar was high priest, and ate the showbread, which it is not lawful to eat save for the priests, and gave also to them that were with him?* [27] *And he said unto them, The sabbath was made for man, and not man for the sabbath:* [28] *so that the Son of man is lord even of the sabbath.*

The sabbath was made for man
Not man for the sabbath

Was God made for us as well?
Where do rules begin?

Does God want to be worshipped?
Who invented that idea?

He is complete unto himself
As absolute as air

The laws of gravity
Physics
Chemistry

Black holes
And constellations
Create joy by their very existence

Who decided
Man
Of all occurrences
Should bow down
Before a deity?

Were we not meant
To be who we are
Created
To enjoy the earth
And proceed apace
In all things possible
Commanding compassion
Allowing love

What else
Is worth considering?

Close down the churches
The temples
And the synagogues
Acknowledge
We are born of light

Isn't that enough?

Remember
We were made
To talk back to idols
Never surrendering to fantasies
Of distant gods

In the greater
And the lesser
Scheme of things
We remain the controversial
And contrary race

Is not that
The best of us?

THE APOSTLES

John 1:35–42

[35] Again on the morrow John was standing, and two of his disciples; [36] and he looked upon Jesus as he walked, and saith, Behold, the Lamb of God! [37] And the two disciples heard him speak, and they followed Jesus. [38] And Jesus turned, and beheld them following, and saith unto them, What seek ye? And they said unto him, Rabbi (which is to say, being interpreted, Teacher), where abidest thou? [39] He saith unto them, Come, and ye shall see. They came therefore and saw where he abode; and they abode with him that day: it was about the tenth hour. [40] One of the two that heard John speak, and followed him, was Andrew, Simon Peter's brother. [41] He findeth first his own brother Simon, and saith unto him, We have found the Messiah (which is, being interpreted, Christ). [42] He brought him unto Jesus. Jesus looked upon him, and said, Thou art Simon the son of John: thou shalt be called Cephas (which is by interpretation, Peter).

We once found the Messiah
Where is he now?

These days
We wait for UFOs to land
Another aborted mythology

In the meantime
The Lamb of God
The Alpha
And the Omega

Lives
At the center of sacrifice

We pray daily
For our unknowing
And our ignorance

The Anunaki
Sky gods
Arrived from the Pleiades
Or maybe the Dog Star
It is claimed
By channelers
Illiterates left behind
And assorted schizophrenics

Like most deities
Who disappeared
They said they'd come again

Gods would seem upon us now
Crop circles revealing higher mathematics
The laser too
Algorithms
DNA

Who is this Savior?
Undoubtedly
Half-man
Half-god
Like other messiahs
Osiris
Isis
Overseers of our phantasmagorica

In the meantime
All this Jesus talks about
Is love and compassion
Forgiveness
Turning the other cheek
Visiting the sick
Nothing conspiratorial

Do we need a God to speak the obvious?

Apparently so

PHILIP AND NATHANAEL

John 1:43–51

⁴³ On the morrow he was minded to go forth into Galilee, and he findeth Philip: and Jesus saith unto him, Follow me. ⁴⁴ Now Philip was from Bethsaida, of the city of Andrew and Peter. ⁴⁵ Philip findeth Nathanael, and saith unto him, We have found him, of whom Moses in the law, and the prophets, wrote, Jesus of Nazareth, the son of Joseph. ⁴⁶ And Nathanael said unto him, Can any good thing come out of Nazareth? Philip saith unto him, Come and see. ⁴⁷ Jesus saw Nathanael coming to him, and saith of him, Behold, an Israelite indeed, in whom is no guile! ⁴⁸ Nathanael saith unto him, Whence knowest thou me? Jesus answered and said unto him, Before Philip called thee, when thou wast under the fig tree, I saw thee. ⁴⁹ Nathanael answered him, Rabbi, thou art the Son of God; thou art King of Israel. ⁵⁰ Jesus answered and said unto him, Because I said unto thee, I saw thee underneath the fig tree, believest thou? thou shalt see greater things than these. ⁵¹ And he saith unto him, Verily, verily, I say unto you, Ye shall see the heaven opened, and the angels of God ascending and descending upon the Son of man.

Can any good come out of Nazareth?
For that matter
Hamtramck
What about Watts
Or anonymous mud flats
And falling down shanties
Scattered everywhere
Across the globe?

Behold!
Jesus promises
Heaven will open up
And angels will descend on him

What about the rest of us?
Do we get angels too
To carry us from the night of our own making
And the common earth where we were born?

Must we pass away
To see pillars of light
Informing us
The Messiah has arrived?

Our ancestors believed in fairy tales
Monsters and leprechauns
Hobbits and gods
Happy endings
For Little Red Riding Hood
Snow White
Harry Potter
Bedtime stories moored in pain
And wondering

Here we have Jesus
Not sure what he's up to
Something about
The King of Israel
These days a claim
Remote
And difficult to understand

We worship gods at a distance
Sometimes on Sunday

Taking their word
They come from light
And deliverance

What does that say about them?

What does that say about us?

WATER INTO WINE

John 2:1–11

¹ *And the third day there was a marriage in Cana of Galilee; and the mother of Jesus was there:* ² *and Jesus also was bidden, and his disciples, to the marriage.* ³ *And when the wine failed, the mother of Jesus saith unto him, They have no wine.* ⁴ *And Jesus saith unto her, Woman, what have I to do with thee? mine hour is not yet come.* ⁵ *His mother saith unto the servants, Whatsoever he saith unto you, do it.* ⁶ *Now there were six waterpots of stone set there after the Jews' manner of purifying, containing two or three firkins apiece.* ⁷ *Jesus saith unto them, Fill the waterpots with water. And they filled them up to the brim.* ⁸ *And he saith unto them, Draw out now, and bear unto the ruler of the feast. And they bare it.* ⁹ *And when the ruler of the feast tasted the water now become wine, and knew not whence it was (but the servants that had drawn the water knew), the ruler of the feast calleth the bridegroom,* ¹⁰ *and saith unto him, Every man setteth on first the good wine; and when men have drunk freely, then that which is worse: thou hast kept the good wine until now.* ¹¹ *This beginning of his signs did Jesus in Cana of Galilee, and manifested his glory; and his disciples believed on him.*

At a wedding running out of wine
He changes water into pinot noir
Or was it Chateauneuf de Pape?

Could they not have ordered in Jamaican rum
Or *uisce*, the water of life?
What about poteen
Hooch

Thunderbird
Or even Mountain Dew?

His mother made him do it
His hour had not yet come
He said

Not to worry
Neither has ours
We wait on wondering
Alcohol the least of it

What we've got
Is what we've got

Time for transformation
Of ordinary time and place
Of drought
And dying dogs
Why
Because we say so
Our only power unconditional love
As if that were possible
Except in self-help books
And dreams

What are we doing here?
Why do we need a Messiah?

What about the Friends of Bill?
First step: powerless over night
And nothingness

Wine won't do it
Neither will miracles

Be still
And listen
To the wind
Within

And the power
Of the naked, unprotected heart

A HOUSE DIVIDED

Mark 3:20–25

²⁰ *And the multitude cometh together again, so that they could not so much as eat bread.* ²¹ *And when his friends heard it, they went out to lay hold on him: for they said, He is beside himself.* ²² *And the scribes that came down from Jerusalem said, He hath Beelzebub, and, By the prince of the demons casteth he out the demons.* ²³ *And he called them unto him, and said unto them in parables, How can Satan cast out Satan?* ²⁴ *And if a kingdom be divided against itself, that kingdom cannot stand.* ²⁵ *And if a house be divided against itself, that house will not be able to stand.*

A house divided cannot stand
Sounds sensible
Does it not?

Two millennia down the pike
This house is still divided
Our brains constructed
To fight
Argue
Massacre each other
On the slightest pretext
And the least offense

The quarrel among ourselves
Takes us down
And pours us out

Upon the commonweal
Dissolving into acrimony
And cries of pain

Jesus promises
He will put us back together again
Casting out the devils
We hold fast within ourselves

Perhaps we prefer
Our taste of evil
Our rapier wit
Our modest revenge
Anything
To shield us
From the blinding light
Of a universe unleashed

THE CLEANSING OF THE TEMPLE

John 2:13–25

¹³ *And the passover of the Jews was at hand, and Jesus went up to Jerusalem.* ¹⁴ *And he found in the temple those that sold oxen and sheep and doves, and the changers of money sitting:* ¹⁵ *and he made a scourge of cords, and cast all out of the temple, both the sheep and the oxen; and he poured out the changers' money, and overthrew their tables;* ¹⁶ *and to them that sold the doves he said, Take these things hence; make not my Father's house a house of merchandise.* ¹⁷ *His disciples remembered that it was written, Zeal for thy house shall eat me up.* ¹⁸ *The Jews therefore answered and said unto him, What sign showest thou unto us, seeing that thou doest these things?* ¹⁹ *Jesus answered and said unto them, Destroy this temple, and in three days I will raise it up.* ²⁰ *The Jews therefore said, Forty and six years was this temple in building, and wilt thou raise it up in three days?* ²¹ *But he spake of the temple of his body.* ²² *When therefore he was raised from the dead, his disciples remembered that he spake this; and they believed the scripture, and the word which Jesus had said.*

²³ *Now when he was in Jerusalem at the passover, during the feast, many believed on his name, beholding his signs which he did.* ²⁴ *But Jesus did not trust himself unto them, for that he knew all men,* ²⁵ *and because he needed not that any one should bear witness concerning man; for he himself knew what was in man.*

Why would Jesus clear the temple court?
Was he borderline?
Whipping sheep
And doves

Driving them out
In a fit of hysteria
What did they ever do
To anyone?

Except be sold for sacrifice
Apparently
The priests or the sellers
Whoever they are
Making a living
From holy wars
And guilt

We still have disadvantages
Among ourselves
We the holy aborigines of Earth

Even Oxford graduates
Operate the sex trade
Opioids
And guns

Surrendering innocence
For coin

How else
To fund the second house
The prep school?
How else Malibu
Vail
And Sutton Place?

Jesus overwrought and overworked
Nobody stopped him
Why was that?

This story doesn't wash

The storyteller here
Detests the business world
Great guilt over currency
The Puritan inheritance
No doubt

Cf. bitcoins
The stock exchange
Commodities

Something
About heights
And depths
Of profit and loss
Scared of the night
And the blinding light

Jesus didn't get out much

An everyday phenomenon
It appears
Among prophets
And seers

NICODEMUS

John 3:1–7

¹ *Now there was a man of the Pharisees, named Nicodemus, a ruler of the Jews:* ² *the same came unto him by night, and said to him, Rabbi, we know that thou art a teacher come from God; for no one can do these signs that thou doest, except God be with him.* ³ *Jesus answered and said unto him, Verily, verily, I say unto thee, Except one be born anew, he cannot see the kingdom of God.* ⁴ *Nicodemus saith unto him, How can a man be born when he is old? can he enter a second time into his mother's womb, and be born?* ⁵ *Jesus answered, Verily, verily, I say unto thee, Except one be born of water and the Spirit, he cannot enter into the kingdom of God.* ⁶ *That which is born of the flesh is flesh; and that which is born of the Spirit is spirit.* ⁷ *Marvel not that I said unto thee, Ye must be born anew.*

Except one be born
Of water and the Spirit
He cannot enter into the kingdom of God

Is that true?
Does anyone dare talk back?

Did the Reformation
Come and go?
How so?
Who puts these claims
In the mouth of the Master?

Sounds like the churches

And the One True Church
The conference of
Bishops
Councils of ministers
Deacons
Priests
Even altar boys
Got together
And went to town

You can't grow up
Until you grasp
You're more than
A case history
Created by your parents
And your past

Born again in the Spirit
Right

I don't know anyone
Baptized
Or not
Who has yet to enter
The Kingdom of God

The greater truth:
Unless you die
Goodbye
You cannot enter Make-Believe

Die to self-absorption
Me
Self-interest
Me

Me
Again more me

That includes
The Council of Churches
And the Vatican
Higher powers by design
And sometimes subterfuge

Look them up

And consider
The meaning of your soul

ABOUT JESUS

John 3:22–36

²² *After these things came Jesus and his disciples into the land of Judæa; and there he tarried with them, and baptized.* ²³ *And John also was baptizing in Ænon near to Salim, because there was much water there: and they W were baptized.* ²⁴ *For John was not yet cast into prison.* ²⁵ *There arose therefore a questioning on the part of John's disciples with a Jew about purifying.* ²⁶ *And they came unto John, and said to him, Rabbi, he that was with thee beyond the Jordan, to whom thou hast borne witness, behold, the same baptizeth, and all men come to him.* ²⁷ *John answered and said, A man can receive nothing, except it have been given him from heaven.* ²⁸ *Ye yourselves bear me witness, that I said, I am not the Christ, but, that I am sent before him.* ²⁹ *He that hath the bride is the bridegroom: but the friend of the bridegroom, that standeth and heareth him, rejoiceth greatly because of the bridegroom's voice: this my joy therefore is made full.* ³⁰ *He must increase, but I must decrease.*

³¹ *He that cometh from above is above all: he that is of the earth is of the earth, and of the earth he speaketh: he that cometh from heaven is above all.* ³² *What he hath seen and heard, of that he beareth witness; and no man receiveth his witness.* ³³ *He that hath received his witness hath set his seal to this, that God is true.* ³⁴ *For he whom God hath sent speaketh the words of God: for he giveth not the Spirit by measure.* ³⁵ *The Father loveth the Son, and hath given all things into his hand.* ³⁶ *He that believeth on the Son hath eternal life; but he that obeyeth not the Son shall not see life, but the wrath of God abideth on him.*

Do you come from heaven?
Or from earth?
Is there a choice?

Why are we invariably
Consistently
Predictably
Split in two?

Who asks the question
Are you sent from God?

Sent for what?
The imagination reels

Choose Jesus
The message says
Or you will surely feel God's wrath

Is this what the Incas
The Aztecs
The Aboriginals
The Inuit
The Muslims chose?

Jesus Christ?

Is this what the Jews
Of all people
Had to listen to
Over the millennia
At the risk of property
And their children's lives?

Where is the poetry
In this relentless prose?
This literal death?
This wholesale propaganda?

All Jesus
Preached was
Love your neighbor
Unconditionally

Sounds too much
Like a greeting card
Doesn't it?

Someone stole the story
And killed the messenger
Someone political
Someone with a large portfolio

Our sorrows flow like rivers
Into the heart of god
Proclaimed the rabbi
Who knew of what he spoke

The imams wept
Mourning followed suit
The high priests sighed
Buddhist nuns
Gamboled in the sun
Praising the universe

Shamans
Various in their moods
Nevertheless
Blessed the rest of us

Oy vey

Oy vey gevalt

THE SAMARITAN WOMAN

John 4:1–42

¹ *When therefore the Lord knew that the Pharisees had heard that Jesus was making and baptizing more disciples than John* ² *(although Jesus himself baptized not, but his disciples),* ³ *he left Judæa, and departed again into Galilee.* ⁴ *And he must needs pass through Samaria.* ⁵ *So he cometh to a city of Samaria, called Sychar, near to the parcel of ground that Jacob gave to his son Joseph:* ⁶ *and Jacob's well was there. Jesus therefore, being wearied with his journey, sat thus by the well. It was about the sixth hour.* ⁷ *There cometh a woman of Samaria to draw water: Jesus saith unto her, Give me to drink.* ⁸ *For his disciples were gone away into the city to buy food.* ⁹ *The Samaritan woman therefore saith unto him, How is it that thou, being a Jew, askest drink of me, who am a Samaritan woman? (For Jews have no dealings with Samaritans.)* ¹⁰ *Jesus answered and said unto her, If thou knewest the gift of God, and who it is that saith to thee, Give me to drink; thou wouldest have asked of him, and he would have given thee living water.* ¹¹ *The woman saith unto him, Sir, thou hast nothing to draw with, and the well is deep: whence then hast thou that living water?* ¹² *Art thou greater than our father Jacob, who gave us the well, and drank thereof himself, and his sons, and his cattle?* ¹³ *Jesus answered and said unto her, Every one that drinketh of this water shall thirst again:* ¹⁴ *but whosoever drinketh of the water that I shall give him shall never thirst; but the water that I shall give him shall become in him a well of water springing up unto eternal life.* ¹⁵ *The woman saith unto him, Sir, give me this water, that I thirst not, neither come all the way hither to draw.* ¹⁶ *Jesus saith unto her, Go, call thy husband, and come hither.* ¹⁷ *The woman answered and said unto him, I have no husband. Jesus saith unto her, Thou saidst well, I have no husband:* ¹⁸ *for thou hast had five husbands; and he whom thou now hast is*

not thy husband: this hast thou said truly. ¹⁹ *The woman saith unto him, Sir, I perceive that thou art a prophet.* ²⁰ *Our fathers worshipped in this mountain; and ye say, that in Jerusalem is the place where men ought to worship.* ²¹ *Jesus saith unto her, Woman, believe me, the hour cometh, when neither in this mountain, nor in Jerusalem, shall ye worship the Father.* ²² *Ye worship that which ye know not: we worship that which we know; for salvation is from the Jews.* ²³ *But the hour cometh, and now is, when the true worshippers shall worship the Father in spirit and truth: for such doth the Father seek to be his worshippers.* ²⁴ *God is a Spirit: and they that worship him must worship in spirit and truth.* ²⁵ *The woman saith unto him, I know that Messiah cometh (he that is called Christ): when he is come, he will declare unto us all things.* ²⁶ *Jesus saith unto her, I that speak unto thee am he.*

²⁷ *And upon this came his disciples; and they marvelled that he was speaking with a woman; yet no man said, What seekest thou? or, Why speakest thou with her?* ²⁸ *So the woman left her waterpot, and went away into the city, and saith to the people,* ²⁹ *Come, see a man, who told me all things that ever I did: can this be the Christ?* ³⁰ *They went out of the city, and were coming to him.* ³¹ *In the mean while the disciples prayed him, saying, Rabbi, eat.* ³² *But he said unto them, I have meat to eat that ye know not.* ³³ *The disciples therefore said one to another, Hath any man brought him aught to eat?* ³⁴ *Jesus saith unto them, My meat is to do the will of him that sent me, and to accomplish his work.* ³⁵ *Say not ye, There are yet four months, and then cometh the harvest? behold, I say unto you, Lift up your eyes, and look on the fields, that they are white already unto harvest.* ³⁶ *He that reapeth receiveth wages, and gathereth fruit unto life eternal; that he that soweth and he that reapeth may rejoice together.* ³⁷ *For herein is the saying true, One soweth, and another reapeth.* ³⁸ *I sent you to reap that whereon ye have not labored: others have labored, and ye are entered into their labor.*

³⁹ *And from that city many of the Samaritans believed on him because of the word of the woman, who testified, He told me all things that ever I did.* ⁴⁰ *So when the Samaritans came unto him, they besought him to abide with them: and he abode there two days.* ⁴¹ *And many more believed because of*

his word; [42] *and they said to the woman, Now we believe, not because of thy speaking: for we have heard for ourselves, and know that this is indeed the Saviour of the world.*

Do we worship a prophet
Standing on a mountaintop?

Do we pay attention to his words?
And in listening
Transform our DNA

Transcending tribe
Clan and spouse
Leaving lovers in the dust
We embrace the human race
Finding God
Where he survives
Doubling down
In unrestricted love

Beggars
Hooker
Druggies
Homeless
Also impossible socialites
Enthralled
With their portfolios

Not to mention hangers on
Obedient staff
Ass-kissing flunkies
Even those with PhDs
All of the above
Impressed with

Celebrity
And loot
The list goes on

In a word
Welcome
To the human throng

What good does it do you
If you only love those
Who love themselves?

Who said that?

God is spirit
The spirit of love
Revealed in flesh
That's us

Imagine that

THE CENTURION'S SON

John 4:43–54

⁴³ *And after the two days he went forth from thence into Galilee.* ⁴⁴ *For Jesus himself testified, that a prophet hath no honor in his own country.* ⁴⁵ *So when he came into Galilee, the Galilæans received him, having seen all the things that he did in Jerusalem at the feast: for they also went unto the feast.*

⁴⁶ *He came therefore again unto Cana of Galilee, where he made the water wine. And there was a certain nobleman, whose son was sick at Capernaum.* ⁴⁷ *When he heard that Jesus was come out of Judæa into Galilee, he went unto him, and besought him that he would come down, and heal his son; for he was at the point of death.* ⁴⁸ *Jesus therefore said unto him, Except ye see signs and wonders, ye will in no wise believe.* ⁴⁹ *The nobleman saith unto him, Sir, come down ere my child die.* ⁵⁰ *Jesus saith unto him, Go thy way; thy son liveth. The man believed the word that Jesus spake unto him, and he went his way.* ⁵¹ *And as he was now going down, his servants met him, saying, that his son lived.* ⁵² *So he inquired of them the hour when he began to amend. They said therefore unto him, Yesterday at the seventh hour the fever left him.* ⁵³ *So the father knew that it was at that hour in which Jesus said unto him, Thy son liveth: and himself believed, and his whole house.* ⁵⁴ *This is again the second sign that Jesus did, having come out of Judæa into Galilee.*

What permission is given
For healing?

Sounds simple enough

73

Mary Baker Eddy
Famously proclaimed
We rest our hope and Faith on God
The only Life, Truth, and Love

Shutting the door on
Cardiologists
Pulmonologists
Internists
Dermatologists
How about penicillin?
Morphine?
Crystal meth?
Just kidding
Pilates anyone?

Some withhold wholeness from themselves
Some embrace their illnesses
Some take pills
Some drink excessively
Some despair

In the end
Eventually
Some find
Their chi
Their flow

Some confront their obstacles
And their love of suffering

Some get well
Or well enough

Could that be us?

Praise God
From whom all blessings flow

THE AUTHORITY OF THE SON

John 5:9–29

⁹ *Now it was the sabbath on that day.* ¹⁰ *So the Jews said unto him that was cured, It is the sabbath, and it is not lawful for thee to take up thy bed.* ¹¹ *But he answered them, He that made me whole, the same said unto me, Take up thy bed, and walk.* ¹² *They asked him, Who is the man that said unto thee, Take up thy bed, and walk?* ¹³ *But he that was healed knew not who it was; for Jesus had conveyed himself away, a multitude being in the place.* ¹⁴ *Afterward Jesus findeth him in the temple, and said unto him, Behold, thou art made whole: sin no more, lest a worse thing befall thee.* ¹⁵ *The man went away, and told the Jews that it was Jesus who had made him whole.* ¹⁶ *And for this cause the Jews persecuted Jesus, because he did these things on the sabbath.* ¹⁷ *But Jesus answered them, My Father worketh even until now, and I work.* ¹⁸ *For this cause therefore the Jews sought the more to kill him, because he not only brake the sabbath, but also called God his own Father, making himself equal with God.*

¹⁹ *Jesus therefore answered and said unto them, Verily, verily, I say unto you, The Son can do nothing of himself, but what he seeth the Father doing: for what things soever he doeth, these the Son also doeth in like manner.* ²⁰ *For the Father loveth the Son, and showeth him all things that himself doeth: and greater works than these will he show him, that ye may marvel.* ²¹ *For as the Father raiseth the dead and giveth them life, even so the Son also giveth life to whom he will.* ²² *For neither doth the Father judge any man, but he hath given all judgment unto the Son;* ²³ *that all may honor the Son, even as they honor the Father. He that honoreth not the Son honoreth not the Father that sent him.* ²⁴ *Verily, verily, I say unto you, He that heareth my word, and believeth him that sent me, hath eternal life, and cometh not into judgment, but hath passed out of death into*

life. ²⁵ Verily, verily, I say unto you, The hour cometh, and now is, when the dead shall hear the voice of the Son of God; and they that hear shall live. ²⁶ For as the Father hath life in himself, even so gave he to the Son also to have life in himself: ²⁷ and he gave him authority to execute judgment, because he is a son of man. ²⁸ Marvel not at this: for the hour cometh, in which all that are in the tombs shall hear his voice, ²⁹ and shall come forth; they that have done good, unto the resurrection of life; and they that have done evil, unto the resurrection of judgment.

They who have done good things
Looking out for the least of these
Assuredly
Will rise from their sepulchers
To cha cha cha on Mardi Gras
And f**k in the meadowland

Those who do evil
Will awaken
Only to be condemned
It says so in the holy book
Oh yes?

Will these risings be silent
And unseen?
Just asking here

Once more
We question
Our higher power

Why is rich and famous
In this land of notoriety
What we are living for?

Why does glamour disappoint
Like heroin
And fentanyl?

There is never enough fame
Never enough celebrity

Hunger for money
Consumes
Our carcasses
Convolutes our innards
Twists our minds

Then
This Jesus
Out of a hundred versions of himself
Advises us to fix on God

God
Silent

Wondrous

And invisible

BETHESDA

John 5:1–15

² Now there is in Jerusalem by the sheep gate a pool, which is called in Hebrew Bethesda, having five porches. ³ In these lay a multitude of them that were sick, blind, halt, withered*. ⁴

¹ After these things there was a feast of the Jews; and Jesus went up to Jerusalem.

² Now there is in Jerusalem by the sheep gate a pool, which is called in Hebrew Bethesda, having five porches. ³ In these lay a multitude of them that were sick, blind, halt, withered. ⁴ †
⁵ And a certain man was there, who had been thirty and eight years in his infirmity. ⁶ When Jesus saw him lying, and knew that he had been now a long time in that case, he saith unto him, Wouldest thou be made whole? ⁷ The sick man answered him, Sir, I have no man, when the water is troubled, to put me into the pool: but while I am coming, another steppeth down before me. ⁸ Jesus saith unto him, Arise, take up thy bed, and walk. ⁹ And straightway the man was made whole, and took up his bed and walked. Now it was the sabbath on that day. ¹⁰ So the Jews said unto him that was cured, It is the sabbath, and it is not lawful for thee to take up thy bed. ¹¹ But he answered them, He that made me whole, the same said unto me, Take up thy bed, and walk. ¹² They asked him, Who is the man that said unto thee, Take up thy bed, and walk? ¹³ But he that was healed knew not who it was; for Jesus had conveyed himself away, a multitude being in the place. ¹⁴ Afterward Jesus findeth him in the temple, and said unto him, Behold, thou art made whole: sin no more, lest a worse thing befall thee. ¹⁵ The man went away, and told the Jews that it was Jesus who had made him whole.

² *Now there is in Jerusalem by the sheep gate a pool, which is called in Hebrew Bethesda, having five porches.* ³ *In these lay a multitude of them that were sick, blind, halt, withered*.* ⁴

Take up your bed and walk

Do we read the Gospels
To be granted permission
For what we already know?
Do we need a green light to grow?

These days
We seem to be surrounded
By friends and lovers
Brought low by infirmity
The politically correct
Euphemistic term
For strokes, cancer, diabetes,
Dementia, heart attacks
Addiction, accidents
Despair

Can Jesus make us whole again
Dare we ask?

Or do we argue incessantly
About the death of God
And the pontification
Of preachers with too many theological degrees?

With evangelical know-it-alls
There are
No questions
No complications

Revelation is complete
We need but surrender to Jesus
Presumably alive and well
Waiting to hear from us

Take up thy bed and walk

Try it
Before you complain
About the death of humankind

If despite everything
You cannot walk again
Then what again?

Where is Jesus then?

² Now there is in Jerusalem by the sheep gate a pool, which is called in Hebrew Bethesda, having five porches. ³ In these lay a multitude of them that were sick, blind, halt, withered*. ⁴ †
⁵ And a certain man was there, who had been thirty and eight years in his infirmity. ⁶ When Jesus saw him lying, and knew that he had been now a long time in that case, he saith unto him, Wouldest thou be made whole? ⁷ The sick man answered him, Sir, I have no man, when the water is troubled, to put me into the pool: but while I am coming, another steppeth down before me. ⁸ Jesus saith unto him, Arise, take up thy bed, and walk. ⁹ And straightway the man was made whole, and took up his bed and walked.

Now it was the sabbath on that day. ¹⁰ So the Jews said unto him that was cured, It is the sabbath, and it is not lawful for thee to take up thy bed. ¹¹ But he answered them, He that made me whole, the same said unto me, Take up thy bed, and walk. ¹² They asked him, Who is the man that said unto thee, Take up thy bed, and walk? ¹³ But he that was healed knew not who it was; for Jesus had conveyed himself away, a multitude being in the place. ¹⁴ Afterward Jesus findeth him in the temple, and said unto him, Behold, thou art made whole: sin no more, lest a worse thing befall thee. ¹⁵ The man went away, and told the Jews that it was Jesus who had made him whole.

² Now there is in Jerusalem by the sheep gate a pool, which is called in Hebrew Bethesda, having five porches. ³ In these lay a multitude of them that were sick, blind, halt, withered*. ⁴

REJECTION IN NAZARETH

Luke 4:16–30

¹⁶ *And he came to Nazareth, where he had been brought up: and he entered, as his custom was, into the synagogue on the sabbath day, and stood up to read.* ¹⁷ *And there was delivered unto him the book of the prophet Isaiah. And he opened the book, and found the place where it was written,*

> ¹⁸ *The Spirit of the Lord is upon me,*
> *Because he anointed me to preach good tidings to the poor:*
> *He hath sent me to proclaim release to the captives,*
> *And recovering of sight to the blind,*
> *To set at liberty them that are bruised,*
> ¹⁹ *To proclaim the acceptable year of the Lord.*

²⁰ *And he closed the book, and gave it back to the attendant, and sat down: and the eyes of all in the synagogue were fastened on him.* ²¹ *And he began to say unto them, To-day hath this scripture been fulfilled in your ears.* ²² *And all bare him witness, and wondered at the words of grace which proceeded out of his mouth: and they said, Is not this Joseph's son?* ²³ *And he said unto them, Doubtless ye will say unto me this parable, Physician, heal thyself: whatsoever we have heard done at Capernaum, do also here in thine own country.* ²⁴ *And he said, Verily I say unto you, No prophet is acceptable in his own country.* ²⁵ *But of a truth I say unto you, There were many widows in Israel in the days of Elijah, when the heaven was shut up three years and six months, when there came a great famine over all the land;* ²⁶ *and unto none of them was Elijah sent, but only to Zarephath, in the land of Sidon, unto a woman that was a widow.* ²⁷ *And there were many lepers in Israel in the time of Elisha the prophet; and none of them was cleansed, but only Naaman the Syrian.* ²⁸ *And they were all filled with wrath in the synagogue, as they heard these things;* ²⁹ *and they rose up,*

and cast him forth out of the city, and led him unto the brow of the hill whereon their city was built, that they might throw him down headlong. [30] *But he passing through the midst of them went his way.*

He proclaims good tidings to the poor
Which means what?
A guaranteed minimum wage?

Freedom for the prisoners
Thieves and murderers presumably?

He orders the blind to recover their sight
Does he overlook the deaf?
What about the amputees?
Where are we going
With these improbable beliefs?

No wonder the townspeople threw him out

We are here immured in flesh
Defined by matter
And pursuits corporeal

Is that not true?

Think again:
Was it God who made us
For a hostile universe?

When we worked to tame
Winds and hurricanes
And eliminate the carnivores
And predatory beasts

They said
We were ruining the earth

When we cut roads through mountains
And dredged the deep
We were told
We despoiled the land

As we forgive those
Who trespass against us

Do we now?

Love the Lord Thy God
With thy whole heart
He says
And thy neighbor as thyself
That's the prescription drug
The ticket to paradise

How then do we heal ourselves?

We are more than wounded
Beyond bruised
We are torn to pieces
Longing to be whole again

Some days our physicians talk too much
At other times our prophets disappear

We sit in silence
And wonderment
Without words
Our brains erased

As we listen to platitudes
About the poor

In the meantime
We are waiting
For the mercy of the universe

And the healing

To come

JESUS BEGINS TO PREACH

Matthew 4:12–22

¹² Now when he heard that John was delivered up, he withdrew into Galilee; ¹³ and leaving Nazareth, he came and dwelt in Capernaum, which is by the sea, in the borders of Zebulun and Naphtali: ¹⁴ that it might be fulfilled which was spoken through Isaiah the prophet, saying,

> *¹⁵ The land of Zebulun and the land of Naphtali,*
> *Toward the sea, beyond the Jordan,*
> *Galilee of the Gentiles,*
> *¹⁶ The people that sat in darkness*
> *Saw a great light,*
> *And to them that sat in the region and shadow of death,*
> *To them did light spring up.*

¹⁷ From that time began Jesus to preach, and to say, Repent ye; for the kingdom of heaven is at hand.

¹⁸ And walking by the sea of Galilee, he saw two brethren, Simon who is called Peter, and Andrew his brother, casting a net into the sea; for they were fishers. ¹⁹ And he saith unto them, Come ye after me, and I will make you fishers of men. ²⁰ And they straightway left the nets, and followed him. ²¹ And going on from thence he saw two other brethren, James the son of Zebedee, and John his brother, in the boat with Zebedee their father, mending their nets; and he called them. ²² And they straightway left the boat and their father, and followed him.

In the shadow of death
A light has dawned
So says holy writ

Where was that light in the Gulag
In Bergen-Belsen
Salem
Cusco
Mexico City
Andersonville
And a thousand ports of call
Of missionary
Or was it mercenary hearts?

After Chartres
Notre Dame
And the beehive huts in Kerry
After Hagia Sofia
And the Cathedral at Rouen
Testaments to passionate belief

Were they but beauty calling out
To the pitiless void?

Inevitable questions linger
And metastasize

How much light did it take
That day in Capernaum
And Galilee?
How much soul
Sent directly from God
For transformation to take place?

After how many Holy Communions
Insistent Confessions
Last Rites
To illuminate
The army of Cortes

The Klan
The SS
The Stasi
The locked wards at Bellevue
Alcatraz
Where is this light we talk about?

We push on the unsuspecting
Telling them to repent
To beg for forgiveness
To die in the arms of the Christ

And still the darkness rules

I am the only one
Who cannot see the light?

THE BEATITUDES

Matthew 5:1–17

¹ *And seeing the multitudes, he went up into the mountain: and when he had sat down, his disciples came unto him:* ² *and he opened his mouth and taught them, saying,*

³ *Blessed are the poor in spirit: for theirs is the kingdom of heaven.*

⁴ *Blessed are they that mourn: for they shall be comforted.*

⁵ *Blessed are the meek: for they shall inherit the earth.*

⁶ *Blessed are they that hunger and thirst after righteousness: for they shall be filled.*

⁷ *Blessed are the merciful: for they shall obtain mercy.*

⁸ *Blessed are the pure in heart: for they shall see God.*

⁹ *Blessed are the peacemakers: for they shall be called sons of God.*

¹⁰ *Blessed are they that have been persecuted for righteousness' sake: for theirs is the kingdom of heaven.* ¹¹ *Blessed are ye when men shall reproach you, and persecute you, and say all manner of evil against you falsely, for my sake.* ¹² *Rejoice, and be exceeding glad: for great is your reward in heaven: for so persecuted they the prophets that were before you.*

¹³ *Ye are the salt of the earth: but if the salt have lost its savor, wherewith shall it be salted? it is thenceforth good for nothing, but to be cast out and trodden under foot of men.* ¹⁴ *Ye are the light of the world. A city set on a hill cannot be hid.* ¹⁵ *Neither do men light a lamp, and put it under the bushel, but on the stand; and it shineth unto all that are in the house.* ¹⁶ *Even so let your light shine before men; that they may see your good works, and glorify your Father who is in heaven.*

¹⁷ *Think not that I came to destroy the law or the prophets: I came not to destroy, but to fulfil.*

Blessed are the poor in spirit
For theirs is the kingdom of heaven

He said

Plundering our imaginations
As to what that could possibly mean

Putting oneself last no doubt
Not daring to presume
One has a particular destiny
Except to serve others
At all costs
To avoid egomania
The source of addictions
Mental instability
And rage

In the mouths of the anointed
And the appointed
The wisdom keepers
Preach from gilded pulpits
With glad voices
And happy hearts
The good news of salvation

The rest of us are expected to tithe
To preserve clerical ascendancy
In this New Age
Of heaven knows
Anything goes

In the meantime
As the Earth warms
And oceans rise to greet us

I see
Hard Shell Baptists
Softening
Hindus abandoning the Ganges
Sufis whirling into each other's arms
Catholics on all sides
Recovering from centuries
Of theological discourse
In seventeen languages
Laid out
By a hundred Doctors of the Church

All poor in spirit
All lost and overwhelmed by purity

Hey!
Who wrote this beatitude?

BLESSED ARE THOSE WHO MOURN

Matthew 5:1–17

^{1} *And seeing the multitudes, he went up into the mountain: and when he had sat down, his disciples came unto him:* ^{2} *and he opened his mouth and taught them, saying,*

^{3} *Blessed are the poor in spirit: for theirs is the kingdom of heaven.*

^{4} *Blessed are they that mourn: for they shall be comforted.*

^{5} *Blessed are the meek: for they shall inherit the earth.*

^{6} *Blessed are they that hunger and thirst after righteousness: for they shall be filled.*

^{7} *Blessed are the merciful: for they shall obtain mercy.*

^{8} *Blessed are the pure in heart: for they shall see God.*

^{9} *Blessed are the peacemakers: for they shall be called sons of God.*

^{10} *Blessed are they that have been persecuted for righteousness' sake: for theirs is the kingdom of heaven.* ^{11} *Blessed are ye when men shall reproach you, and persecute you, and say all manner of evil against you falsely, for my sake.* ^{12} *Rejoice, and be exceeding glad: for great is your reward in heaven: for so persecuted they the prophets that were before you.*

^{13} *Ye are the salt of the earth: but if the salt have lost its savor, wherewith shall it be salted? it is thenceforth good for nothing, but to be cast out and trodden under foot of men.* ^{14} *Ye are the light of the world. A city set on a hill cannot be hid.* ^{15} *Neither do men light a lamp, and put it under the bushel, but on the stand; and it shineth unto all that are in the house.* ^{16} *Even so let your light shine before men; that they may see your good works, and glorify your Father who is in heaven.*

^{17} *Think not that I came to destroy the law or the prophets: I came not to destroy, but to fulfil.*

Blessed are those who mourn
For they will be comforted

This
A long and overbearing catalogue

Aside from every human who ever lived
Loss our middle name
Let us now praise
The Rohingya of Myanmar
The Jews of Prague
Warsaw
Munich
And Rome
Anywhere there's art and science
Bam

What about the Kulaks
Their crime prosperity
They were probably nouveau riche
Which is famously worse
Dead by the truckloads
Their names erased
From the bureaucracy

Here's to the landowners in Han
The Uyghurs
Unpronounceable
Now dead
How many millions bought the farm
In the Gulags
In Eire beyond the Pale
The list goes on
The Sioux at Little Big Horn
The Ludlow Massacre

Babi Yar
Rumbula
The Rape of Nanking
St. Bartholomew's Day

What about the Akash
Our etheric compendium?
How many dead in the telling?
An elephant never forgets

Who said mourn?

The Trail of Tears outpours the rain
Are we blessed for being merely alive?
No one can separate
The two

Not God

Not you

BLESSED ARE THE MEEK

Matthew 5:1–17

¹ *And seeing the multitudes, he went up into the mountain: and when he had sat down, his disciples came unto him:* ² *and he opened his mouth and taught them, saying,*

³ *Blessed are the poor in spirit: for theirs is the kingdom of heaven.*

⁴ *Blessed are they that mourn: for they shall be comforted.*

⁵ *Blessed are the meek: for they shall inherit the earth.*

⁶ *Blessed are they that hunger and thirst after righteousness: for they shall be filled.*

⁷ *Blessed are the merciful: for they shall obtain mercy.*

⁸ *Blessed are the pure in heart: for they shall see God.*

⁹ *Blessed are the peacemakers: for they shall be called sons of God.*

¹⁰ *Blessed are they that have been persecuted for righteousness' sake: for theirs is the kingdom of heaven.* ¹¹ *Blessed are ye when men shall reproach you, and persecute you, and say all manner of evil against you falsely, for my sake.* ¹² *Rejoice, and be exceeding glad: for great is your reward in heaven: for so persecuted they the prophets that were before you.*

¹³ *Ye are the salt of the earth: but if the salt have lost its savor, wherewith shall it be salted? it is thenceforth good for nothing, but to be cast out and trodden under foot of men.* ¹⁴ *Ye are the light of the world. A city set on a hill cannot be hid.* ¹⁵ *Neither do men light a lamp, and put it under the bushel, but on the stand; and it shineth unto all that are in the house.* ¹⁶ *Even so let your light shine before men; that they may see your good works, and glorify your Father who is in heaven.*

¹⁷ *Think not that I came to destroy the law or the prophets: I came not to destroy, but to fulfil.*

Blessed are the meek
They will inherit the earth

Once again
Believers admonished
To tone down
The rhetoric
The outrage
The anger

The Old Testament inheritance
No doubt

Does this particular beatitude
Address women with loud voices
Transsexuals from nowhere
The out-of-working class
Upstairs maids
These days
Downstairs
In the basement

How does the fabled one percent
Who contribute big to benefits
Train to be meek
And still make a killing?

How meek was Churchill
And Richard III?
What about Lady Macbeth?

The Apostolic establishment
Mystics at every turn
The ordained and educated magisterium
Insist all believers should be meek

Modest

Mild

Compliant

Most especially Muslims
And Jews
Keep it down
Union leaders
Witches
Renegade nuns
And Hollywood czars

Unless they're filming *Quo Vadis*
Or *Spartacus*
In which case
Loud voices are allowed

Blessed are the meek

You first

BLESSED ARE THOSE WHO HUNGER
AND THIRST FOR RIGHTEOUSNESS

Matthew 5:1–17

¹ And seeing the multitudes, he went up into the mountain: and when he had sat down, his disciples came unto him: ² and he opened his mouth and taught them, saying,

³ Blessed are the poor in spirit: for theirs is the kingdom of heaven.

⁴ Blessed are they that mourn: for they shall be comforted.

⁵ Blessed are the meek: for they shall inherit the earth.

⁶ Blessed are they that hunger and thirst after righteousness: for they shall be filled.

⁷ Blessed are the merciful: for they shall obtain mercy.

⁸ Blessed are the pure in heart: for they shall see God.

⁹ Blessed are the peacemakers: for they shall be called sons of God.

¹⁰ Blessed are they that have been persecuted for righteousness' sake: for theirs is the kingdom of heaven. ¹¹ Blessed are ye when men shall reproach you, and persecute you, and say all manner of evil against you falsely, for my sake. ¹² Rejoice, and be exceeding glad: for great is your reward in heaven: for so persecuted they the prophets that were before you.

¹³ Ye are the salt of the earth: but if the salt have lost its savor, wherewith shall it be salted? it is thenceforth good for nothing, but to be cast out and trodden under foot of men. ¹⁴ Ye are the light of the world. A city set on a hill cannot be hid. ¹⁵ Neither do men light a lamp, and put it under the bushel, but on the stand; and it shineth unto all that are in the house. ¹⁶ Even so let your light shine before men; that they may see your good works, and glorify your Father who is in heaven.

¹⁷ Think not that I came to destroy the law or the prophets: I came not to destroy, but to fulfil.

Blessed are those who hunger and thirst for righteousness
For they will be filled

Filled with what?
Fast food?
Fine dining?
Name one person who hungered for righteousness
Who has been filled

In some quarters
Union's still a dirty word
Women's liberation a continuing amusement
Rape the quotidian occupation
That means day by day
In every way

In the meantime
Consider
The righteousness of the land
The sweep of sky
The mother sea
Endangered species struggling to endure
In the face of profit and loss
And ridicule

Those who hunger and thirst for justice
Yes
For righteousness
For balance hey
Will be filled with bureaucracy
Our side and their side
Paralyzed

Told to calm down
Given Clozaril
And sound bites
Yum

And will eventually learn
To be still

And unobtrusively

Survive

Isn't that the way?

BLESSED ARE THE MERCIFUL

Matthew 5:1–17

¹ *And seeing the multitudes, he went up into the mountain: and when he had sat down, his disciples came unto him:* ² *and he opened his mouth and taught them, saying,*

³ *Blessed are the poor in spirit: for theirs is the kingdom of heaven.*

⁴ *Blessed are they that mourn: for they shall be comforted.*

⁵ *Blessed are the meek: for they shall inherit the earth.*

⁶ *Blessed are they that hunger and thirst after righteousness: for they shall be filled.*

⁷ *Blessed are the merciful: for they shall obtain mercy.*

⁸ *Blessed are the pure in heart: for they shall see God.*

⁹ *Blessed are the peacemakers: for they shall be called sons of God.*

¹⁰ *Blessed are they that have been persecuted for righteousness' sake: for theirs is the kingdom of heaven.* ¹¹ *Blessed are ye when men shall reproach you, and persecute you, and say all manner of evil against you falsely, for my sake.* ¹² *Rejoice, and be exceeding glad: for great is your reward in heaven: for so persecuted they the prophets that were before you.*

¹³ *Ye are the salt of the earth: but if the salt have lost its savor, wherewith shall it be salted? it is thenceforth good for nothing, but to be cast out and trodden under foot of men.* ¹⁴ *Ye are the light of the world. A city set on a hill cannot be hid.* ¹⁵ *Neither do men light a lamp, and put it under the bushel, but on the stand; and it shineth unto all that are in the house.* ¹⁶ *Even so let your light shine before men; that they may see your good works, and glorify your Father who is in heaven.*

¹⁷ *Think not that I came to destroy the law or the prophets: I came not to destroy, but to fulfil.*

Blessed are the merciful
For they will be shown mercy

That sounds fine
For judges
Tax collectors
Supreme Court justices
Wardens
Executioners

That said
Are they too ingrained
Too recalcitrant
To be merciful?

What about rapists?
What about the rest of us?

Do we dream
An eye for an eye
A tooth for a tooth
In the face of
Homegrown terrorists
School shooters
Internet predators
Husbands grown weary of wives?

Instead of life imprisonment
With no chance of parole
Be merciful
Give them seventy years
Maybe seventy-five

A chance of parole
Only when they're connected to a feeding tube

What God gives mercy
To the demented
The deranged
The amputees
Brain damaged
Stillborn
Autistic
Damaged
Parts of me?

Ubi gentium summus?

Where in the world are we?

Where are we going?

And when?

BLESSED ARE THE PURE IN HEART

Matthew 5:1–17

[1] *And seeing the multitudes, he went up into the mountain: and when he had sat down, his disciples came unto him:* [2] *and he opened his mouth and taught them, saying,*

[3] *Blessed are the poor in spirit: for theirs is the kingdom of heaven.*

[4] *Blessed are they that mourn: for they shall be comforted.*

[5] *Blessed are the meek: for they shall inherit the earth.*

[6] *Blessed are they that hunger and thirst after righteousness: for they shall be filled.*

[7] *Blessed are the merciful: for they shall obtain mercy.*

[8] *Blessed are the pure in heart: for they shall see God.*

[9] *Blessed are the peacemakers: for they shall be called sons of God.*

[10] *Blessed are they that have been persecuted for righteousness' sake: for theirs is the kingdom of heaven.* [11] *Blessed are ye when men shall reproach you, and persecute you, and say all manner of evil against you falsely, for my sake.* [12] *Rejoice, and be exceeding glad: for great is your reward in heaven: for so persecuted they the prophets that were before you.*

[13] *Ye are the salt of the earth: but if the salt have lost its savor, wherewith shall it be salted? it is thenceforth good for nothing, but to be cast out and trodden under foot of men.* [14] *Ye are the light of the world. A city set on a hill cannot be hid.* [15] *Neither do men light a lamp, and put it under the bushel, but on the stand; and it shineth unto all that are in the house.* [16] *Even so let your light shine before men; that they may see your good works, and glorify your Father who is in heaven.*

[17] *Think not that I came to destroy the law or the prophets: I came not to destroy, but to fulfil.*

Blessed are the pure in heart
For they will see God

Who he is talking about?

These days
Who could be pure?

Do we suggest
Schizophrenia
Down Syndrome?
Autism no doubt
Angels in disguise

In the end
The rest of us seem
Loaded down with funerals
Shattered friendships
Bankrupt hearts

Eventually dementia
The mind erasing light

Again
How else can one be pure?

In this singular set-up
We sell our souls
For a democracy
Girded not by pure intent
Got that?
But by ICBMs
Intercontinental ballistic missiles
Thermonuclear warheads
Minimum range

Fifty-five hundred kilometers
Courtesy of the military state

Fine
Excellent
Reassuring
Yea

We are Machiavellian
Proud in our deception
Proclaiming survival
At all costs
What is the alternative?

All is not lost
We can at least pretend to be pure
And on some level
Know what it feels like
To love the human race
Unconditionally

At least in the movies

Fade Out

Once again

The End

BLESSED ARE THE PEACEMAKERS

Matthew 5:1–17

^{1} *And seeing the multitudes, he went up into the mountain: and when he had sat down, his disciples came unto him:* ^{2} *and he opened his mouth and taught them, saying,*

^{3} *Blessed are the poor in spirit: for theirs is the kingdom of heaven.*

^{4} *Blessed are they that mourn: for they shall be comforted.*

^{5} *Blessed are the meek: for they shall inherit the earth.*

^{6} *Blessed are they that hunger and thirst after righteousness: for they shall be filled.*

^{7} *Blessed are the merciful: for they shall obtain mercy.*

^{8} *Blessed are the pure in heart: for they shall see God.*

^{9} *Blessed are the peacemakers: for they shall be called sons of God.*

^{10} *Blessed are they that have been persecuted for righteousness' sake: for theirs is the kingdom of heaven.* ^{11} *Blessed are ye when men shall reproach you, and persecute you, and say all manner of evil against you falsely, for my sake.* ^{12} *Rejoice, and be exceeding glad: for great is your reward in heaven: for so persecuted they the prophets that were before you.*

^{13} *Ye are the salt of the earth: but if the salt have lost its savor, wherewith shall it be salted? it is thenceforth good for nothing, but to be cast out and trodden under foot of men.* ^{14} *Ye are the light of the world. A city set on a hill cannot be hid.* ^{15} *Neither do men light a lamp, and put it under the bushel, but on the stand; and it shineth unto all that are in the house.* ^{16} *Even so let your light shine before men; that they may see your good works, and glorify your Father who is in heaven.*

^{17} *Think not that I came to destroy the law or the prophets: I came not to destroy, but to fulfil.*

Blessed are the peacemakers
For they shall be called children of God

Consider Dorothy Day
Staring down weapons in Times Square
Got to tell the world
She don't take shit
From Wall Street warriors

Daniel Berrigan
Dumping duck blood
On draft files
Before being dragged to jail

Simone Weil
Perishing from grief
A holy hunger strike
In World War Two

Dietrich Bonhoeffer
No man can change the truth
Executed by the Reich
Why not?

These are the children of light
They won't bow down before Yahweh
War god of the Canaanites

They sit instead
With Jesus
The rabbi carpenter from Nazareth
The Prince of Peace

Before he and his New Testament
Were carried to the battlefield

By either side
Of any argument
To bless war
And state sponsored massacres
Full speed ahead
By Jove

Praise God
And pass the ammunition!

BLESSED ARE THOSE WHO
ARE PERSECUTED

Matthew 5:1–17

¹ And seeing the multitudes, he went up into the mountain: and when he had sat down, his disciples came unto him: ² and he opened his mouth and taught them, saying,

³ Blessed are the poor in spirit: for theirs is the kingdom of heaven.

⁴ Blessed are they that mourn: for they shall be comforted.

⁵ Blessed are the meek: for they shall inherit the earth.

⁶ Blessed are they that hunger and thirst after righteousness: for they shall be filled.

⁷ Blessed are the merciful: for they shall obtain mercy.

⁸ Blessed are the pure in heart: for they shall see God.

⁹ Blessed are the peacemakers: for they shall be called sons of God.

¹⁰ Blessed are they that have been persecuted for righteousness' sake: for theirs is the kingdom of heaven. ¹¹ Blessed are ye when men shall reproach you, and persecute you, and say all manner of evil against you falsely, for my sake. ¹² Rejoice, and be exceeding glad: for great is your reward in heaven: for so persecuted they the prophets that were before you.

¹³ Ye are the salt of the earth: but if the salt have lost its savor, wherewith shall it be salted? it is thenceforth good for nothing, but to be cast out and trodden under foot of men. ¹⁴ Ye are the light of the world. A city set on a hill cannot be hid. ¹⁵ Neither do men light a lamp, and put it under the bushel, but on the stand; and it shineth unto all that are in the house. ¹⁶ Even so let your light shine before men; that they may see your good works, and glorify your Father who is in heaven.

¹⁷ Think not that I came to destroy the law or the prophets: I came not to destroy, but to fulfil.

Blessed are those who are persecuted
Because of righteousness
For theirs is the kingdom of heaven

Kingdom of Heaven?
Are we hard-wired for royalty?
Our Lord?
Prince of Peace?
King of Kings?
In capital letters
Halos
And gold lame?

What about
The Emperor of Ice Cream?
The Princess Bride?
The Prince and the Show Girl?
Does God ever laugh?

In the same breath
He calls us the light of the world
Yes us
You and me
Avoiding persecution
By all means
Convincing ourselves
We are light
When we are awash
In blood
And cannot braille our way
Out of war
And conflagration

The list of the reviled is long
In the collective
And the particular
Rohingya
Uighurs
Mexicans
Women wanting abortions
Men entranced with men
Women with women
Transsexuals unfastening their loins
Whistleblowers crying out to the wind and rain

Persecution
Surely
A by-product of bureaucracy
A misunderstanding
Among people with too many guns

And no doubt
Too many dreams

BLESSED ARE YOU WHEN
PEOPLE INSULT YOU

Matthew 5:1–17

¹ And seeing the multitudes, he went up into the mountain: and when he had sat down, his disciples came unto him: ² and he opened his mouth and taught them, saying,

³ Blessed are the poor in spirit: for theirs is the kingdom of heaven.

⁴ Blessed are they that mourn: for they shall be comforted.

⁵ Blessed are the meek: for they shall inherit the earth.

⁶ Blessed are they that hunger and thirst after righteousness: for they shall be filled.

⁷ Blessed are the merciful: for they shall obtain mercy.

⁸ Blessed are the pure in heart: for they shall see God.

⁹ Blessed are the peacemakers: for they shall be called sons of God.

¹⁰ Blessed are they that have been persecuted for righteousness' sake: for theirs is the kingdom of heaven. ¹¹ Blessed are ye when men shall reproach you, and persecute you, and say all manner of evil against you falsely, for my sake. ¹² Rejoice, and be exceeding glad: for great is your reward in heaven: for so persecuted they the prophets that were before you.

¹³ Ye are the salt of the earth: but if the salt have lost its savor, wherewith shall it be salted? it is thenceforth good for nothing, but to be cast out and trodden under foot of men. ¹⁴ Ye are the light of the world. A city set on a hill cannot be hid. ¹⁵ Neither do men light a lamp, and put it under the bushel, but on the stand; and it shineth unto all that are in the house. ¹⁶ Even so let your light shine before men; that they may see your good works, and glorify your Father who is in heaven.

¹⁷ *Think not that I came to destroy the law or the prophets: I came not to destroy, but to fulfil.*

Blessed are you when people insult you
And persecute you
Because of me
Rejoice and be glad
Your reward is great in heaven

Because of me
He says
Foreshadowing
Christians torn to smithereens
In Nero's Rome

Or what?

Persecution's a two-way street
Insults descending like the dark
Mutilation a multi-cultural opportunity

Innocents reviled
For everything untoward
For being fat
Poor
Short
Promiscuous
Even altogether asexual

Rewards come scant
Unless one becomes a Cardinal
Or owns a television gospel hour
Thank-you Jesus
In which case
You will be provided with an office staff

A publicist
And a PhD in social media

Two thousand years
Past prophets and seers
Sisters of Mercy
And street corner evangelists
Now arrive
Sealed signed and delivered
In fifty-seven varieties

Blessed are you when people insult you
And persecute you
Because of me

Imagining you
And your love of
Atheists
Transsexuals
Prisoners
And possible insurrectionists
None of it rhyming
Discordant hearts
Grasping for meaning
That does not reveal itself

In the meantime
We will serve spaghetti Bolognese
Walk the Labrador
And secure the soccer game

We do not dwell
On tyrants
And torture cells
They will find us soon enough

Paradise comes now

If we wait until later
The dark may find us standing still

And heaven may not come at all

THE SALT OF THE EARTH

Matthew 5:13

[13] *Ye are the salt of the earth: but if the salt have lost its savor, wherewith shall it be salted? it is thenceforth good for nothing, but to be cast out and trodden under foot of men.*

I am drawn to the salt lick
In the middle of the night
To feed with other predators

Monsters we have become
Attacking to survive

I was born
With salt in the blood
And the crippling asides
That pour down like rain

Salt of the earth
My leitmotiv

I can be
Openhearted
And accessible
Except
When I crave carrion flesh

How does one lose one's salt

And one's savour
In an age of hypertension
And oblivion

I am the lion
I am the jackal
I am the asp
I will prevail
If I have to devour you first

Jesus
The rabbi from Nazareth
The carpenter
The crazy one
Troubles me big-time

Justice
Peace
And forgiveness

Is that what I'm here for?

They are so much blathering

I am blood

THE LIGHT OF THE WORLD

Matthew 5:14–16

14 Ye are the light of the world. A city set on a hill cannot be hid. 15 Neither do men light a lamp, and put it under the bushel, but on the stand; and it shineth unto all that are in the house. 16 Even so let your light shine before men; that they may see your good works, and glorify your Father who is in heaven.

Put your light on the mountaintop

Said the rabbi
Said the priest
Said the self-help authority
Ching ching
And my great aunt Edna

Everyone will see my good deeds
And would-be achievements

What for?
Asked the therapist
Complicating the simplest of truths
Scrambling my life
Like supermarket eggs

In the meantime
We are told to shine
This little light of mine

So too the god man says
Do not hide your light
Under a basket

Who would do that?

Jesus offers bromides
Yes
We already know
We've already memorized
What is happening here

In the meantime
We live and die
With metaphor

Light is popular these days

I AM COME TO FULFILL

Matthew 5:17–20

¹⁷ *Think not that I came to destroy the law or the prophets: I came not to destroy, but to fulfil.* ¹⁸ *For verily I say unto you, Till heaven and earth pass away, one jot or one tittle shall in no wise pass away from the law, till all things be accomplished.* ¹⁹ *Whosoever therefore shall break one of these least commandments, and shall teach men so, shall be called least in the kingdom of heaven: but whosoever shall do and teach them, he shall be called great in the kingdom of heaven.* ²⁰ *For I say unto you, that except your righteousness shall exceed the righteousness of the scribes and Pharisees, ye shall in no wise enter into the kingdom of heaven.*

For I tell you
That unless your righteousness
Surpasses that of the Pharisees
You will not enter the kingdom of heaven

That's comforting

Should I consult a scholar
To decipher what that means?

Righteousness
From what I understand
Embraces everyone

With liberty and justice for all

How's that?

We do pay our taxes
Drive under the speed limit
Use deodorant
Are careful with politicians
And minorities

As for the Pharisees
A complicated group
Given to deciphering the law
Good for them

Someone needs to interpret their overall intent

What about entering heaven?
Any clear definition of that?
It all sounds hypothetical

Especially when we've been taught
The meaning of God is love

Especially when we've had it hammered in
Yada yada

Love your neighbor as yourself
Remains
Unsolicited advice
A Hallmark greeting card

Cymbals and sounding brass

What will it take for us
To hit rock bottom

And open up our wicked hearts?

Present company disqualified
That means you and me

Righteous to the end

That's us

MURDER

Matthew 5:21–26

21 Ye have heard that it was said to them of old time, Thou shalt not kill; and whosoever shall kill shall be in danger of the judgment: 22 but I say unto you, that everyone who is angry with his brother shall be in danger of the judgment; and whosoever shall say to his brother, Raca, shall be in danger of the council; and whosoever shall say, Thou fool, shall be in danger of the hell of fire. 23 If therefore thou art offering thy gift at the altar, and there rememberest that thy brother hath aught against thee, 24 leave there thy gift before the altar, and go thy way, first be reconciled to thy brother, and then come and offer thy gift. 25 Agree with thine adversary quickly, while thou art with him in the way; lest haply the adversary deliver thee to the judge, and the judge deliver thee to the officer, and thou be cast into prison. 26 Verily I say unto thee, Thou shalt by no means come out thence, till thou have paid the last farthing.

Jesus says anger becomes
The counterpart of homicide

Anyone who says, "You fool!"
Could land himself
In hell

Oh boy

What about religious war
In the ordinary scheme of things?
What about sodomites

And adulterers?

Who burned the witches
By the way?

Here's to Joan of Arc
She listened
To the angels' whisperings

Here's to so-called heretics
Martin Luther
Socrates
Savonarola
Not to mention
Madalyn Murray O'Hair
American atheist
Prominent among the disappeared

Injunctions
From Jesus
Come across harsh
Did someone stuff words in his mouth?
Predictably so

Here we go
The fabulous Old Testament again
Relentless laws
Directives
Rules

In the meantime
Somebody hijacked
The Prince of Peace

Sweet souls

Suffused with mercy
And benevolence
Seem to unsettle
Responsible people
And levelheaded citizens
Like us

Get me out of here

ADULTERY

Matthew 5:27–30

27 *Ye have heard that it was said, Thou shalt not commit adultery:* 28 *but I say unto you, that every one that looketh on a woman to lust after her hath committed adultery with her already in his heart.* 29 *And if thy right eye causeth thee to stumble, pluck it out, and cast it from thee: for it is profitable for thee that one of thy members should perish, and not thy whole body be cast into hell.* 30 *And if thy right hand causeth thee to stumble, cut it off, and cast it from thee: for it is profitable for thee that one of thy members should perish, and not thy whole body go into hell.*

If your thy right eye causes thee to stumble
Pluck it out and cast it from thee

Say what?

. . . for it is profitable for thee that one of thy members should perish,
and not thy whole body go into hell

Hell again

Hello?

Most of us lack faith in netherworlds
Designed to trap the unsuspecting
And the weak

In any case
Doesn't sound like Jesus Christ

Who put declarations in the Master's mouth?

Somebody's somebody committed adultery
Is that so?
This somebody's getting revenge
Reverting to a creed
About retaliation and revenge

I look to the hills
For clear sky
And relentless wind
Reminding me of the sea
From whence it blew
A place of unremitting green
Almost emerald

Otherwise
Bottomless and black
Depending on the moods
Of Mother Earth

And the storms of humankind
Majestic in their fury
Complete in chaos
Lighting up the universe
With electricity
And fire

And sometimes ecstasy

So much for gouging and dismembering

And hell

THE LORD'S PRAYER

Matthew 6:7–15

⁷ And in praying use not vain repetitions, as the Gentiles do: for they think that they shall be heard for their much speaking. ⁸ Be not therefore like unto them: for your Father knoweth what things ye have need of, before ye ask him. ⁹ After this manner therefore pray ye: Our Father who art in heaven, Hallowed be thy name. ¹⁰ Thy kingdom come. Thy will be done, as in heaven, so on earth. ¹¹ Give us this day our daily bread. ¹² And forgive us our debts, as we also have forgiven our debtors. ¹³ And bring us not into temptation, but deliver us from the evil one. ¹⁴ For if ye forgive men their trespasses, your heavenly Father will also forgive you. ¹⁵ But if ye forgive not men their trespasses, neither will your Father forgive your trespasses.

Why does Jesus
Call God Father
In a world of fathers on the lam
Beyond DNA
And childhood memory?

Fathers incapable of warmth
Especially for themselves
Men beaten down
In mines
Brain dead on assembly lines
Drowned in shipwrecks
And corner bars

Father?

When did fathers sit in heaven?
Hallowed be thy name
Sounds like Halloween
Masks and apparitions of the dead

Forgive us our debts
Really?
As we forgive our debtors
The bankers never do

What about trespassers?
Sounds like burglars
Coming across the yard
Intent on breaking in

We forgive you whoever you are
Don't murder us in the meantime

Deliver us from evil
Especially the wickedness
We inflict on ourselves
Selling us short
Belittling our accomplishments
When all we needed
Was to love ourselves

He says love your enemies
We're not ready for that
Not even close

For thine is the kingdom

Would that include
Buckingham Palace?

Kensington Palace?
Magic Kingdom Disneyworld?

Words get in the way
Of a meaning
That slipped away
Before it was ever known
Or understood

PRAY

Matthew 6:5–6

⁵ And when ye pray, ye shall not be as the hypocrites: for they love to stand and pray in the synagogues and in the corners of the streets, that they may be seen of men. Verily I say unto you, They have received their reward. ⁶ But thou, when thou prayest, enter into thine inner chamber, and having shut thy door, pray to thy Father who is in secret, and thy Father who seeth in secret shall recompense thee.

But thou, when thou prayest, enter into thine inner chamber and having shut thy door, pray to thy Father who is in secret

Says Jesus Christ
The avatar

What about Sundays
11 a.m.?
How about Chartres and Notre Dame?
Not to mention the Vatican
St. Peter's in Chains
St. Patrick's Fifth Avenue
St. Paul's
Christopher Wrenn
The National Cathedral
In Washington DC

Praying in secret?
What's the point?

Are we not interconnected DNA on speed?

Incidentally
When did Jesus shut his door?

Secret prayers are predictable:
Let me live forever
F**k forever
Let me be rich

The Transfiguration a rock concert
The Crucifixion a public spectacle

My God, my God

Why hast thou forsaken me?

The church a grand place for fashion
And microphones
Opera on a planetary scale

My God, my God

Shut up
Les miserables
Keep your misery to yourself

What's the point in secrecy
God loves a carnival
The tumult
The commotion
The hullaballoo

Let us join hands
And shout
Hallelu

Yes
Hallelu

DO NOT WORRY

Matthew 6:25–27

²⁵ *Therefore I say unto you, Be not anxious for your life, what ye shall eat, or what ye shall drink; nor yet for your body, what ye shall put on. Is not the life more than the food, and the body than the raiment?* ²⁶ *Behold the birds of the heaven, that they sow not, neither do they reap, nor gather into barns; and your heavenly Father feedeth them. Are not ye of much more value than they?* ²⁷ *And which of you by being anxious can add one cubit unto the measure of his life?*

Behold the birds of the heaven
That they sow not
Neither do they reap
Nor gather into barns
And your heavenly Father feedeth them

He do

Good advice
To be taken on faith

Accordingly
Do not worry when the rent is due
When crops freeze
Mills shut down
And husbands disappear
Along with child support
And pregnant mistresses

Migrants
In no particular order
Perish in the desert sun
Their children stuffed in cages
Their dreams short-circuited

And which of you by being anxious
can add one cubit unto the measure of his life?

When there's no cash for medical emergencies
People pushed out
Penniless and dispossessed
Properties foreclosed
The near best of us
Expiring from fentanyl and heroin
Remember
Our heavenly Father feeds the birds
And various endangered species
Eagles notwithstanding

What me worry?

Not a chance

LOVE YOUR ENEMIES

Matthew 5:43–48

⁴³ Ye have heard that it was said, Thou shalt love thy neighbor, and hate thine enemy: ⁴⁴ but I say unto you, Love your enemies, and pray for them that persecute you; ⁴⁵ that ye may be sons of your Father who is in heaven: for he maketh his sun to rise on the evil and the good, and sendeth rain on the just and the unjust. ⁴⁶ For if ye love them that love you, what reward have ye? do not even the publicans the same? ⁴⁷ And if ye salute your brethren only, what do ye more than others? do not even the Gentiles the same? ⁴⁸ Ye therefore shall be perfect, as your heavenly Father is perfect.

———————————————————

Love your enemies

Is that so?

How do you love your executioners
Your homegrown hooligans
Who would just as soon see you dead
Until you let go of earth
And ground
And disappear?

Unless you surrender
Into nothingness

Pray for them that persecute you

Why not ignore them?

On the other hand
Why not sue them
And wreck them financially?

Lend to your enemies
Without expecting anything back
He says
Suggesting blueprints for catastrophe

To be blotted out
By one's own hand

Is that the meaning of love?
Wow once again wow

Be perfect
He says

Be best
Says the White House
Redesigning language
And once again
Re-inventing thought

Love your enemies

We need to work on that

Don't you?

JUDGE NOT

Luke 6:37–42

37 And judge not, and ye shall not be judged: and condemn not, and ye shall not be condemned: release, and ye shall be released: 38 give, and it shall be given unto you; good measure, pressed down, shaken together, running over, shall they give into your bosom. For with what measure ye mete it shall be measured to you again.

39 And he spake also a parable unto them, Can the blind guide the blind? shall they not both fall into a pit? 40 The disciple is not above his teacher: but every one when he is perfected shall be as his teacher. 41 And why beholdest thou the mote that is in thy brother's eye, but considerest not the beam that is in thine own eye? 42 Or how canst thou say to thy brother, Brother, let me cast out the mote that is in thine eye, when thou thyself beholdest not the beam that is in thine own eye? Thou hypocrite, cast out first the beam out of thine own eye, and then shalt thou see clearly to cast out the mote that is in thy brother's eye.

Can the blind lead the blind?
A rhetorical consideration
No doubt

Judge not
And ye shall not be judged

Who would judge me?
Only me
This frightened
Disapproving

Specimen
Professing to be whole
Needing nothing
I shout out
Only my own opinion of the universe

Waking up
And lying down
I judge the obvious
Snakes in my garden
Panthers next door
Nazis on the telephone

My tone
One of carefully modulated paranoia

I have perfected several roles:
Salt of the earth
Hale fellow well met
Raconteur

If I'm mean enough
No one will judge me
They will know enough
To stay away
And so will I

Condemn not
And ye shall not be condemned

Condemned for what?

We come with contradictions
We cannot easily escape

Complications arrive uninvited
Infections damage our resolve

Sepsis invades our pores
Black night wrecking us

Before we have learned to love

A TREE AND ITS FRUIT

Luke 6:43–45

[43] For there is no good tree that bringeth forth corrupt fruit; nor again a corrupt tree that bringeth forth good fruit. [44] For each tree is known by its own fruit. For of thorns men do not gather figs, nor of a bramble bush gather they grapes. [45] The good man out of the good treasure of his heart bringeth forth that which is good; and the evil man out of the evil treasure bringeth forth that which is evil: for out of the abundance of the heart his mouth speaketh.

There is no good tree that bringeth forth corrupt fruit

What do we do
With shards of possible intelligence

Except to nod our heads
And pretend
We are somebody else?

Hard to believe
Jesus the carpenter
The rabble-rousing rabbi
Collected maxims
For the masses
After a thousand years of Jewish scholarship

Please tell me
This avatar of light

This holy spirit
This Christed consciousness
Expends more energy
Visualizing the likes of us
As loved
Cherished
And utterly complete

That
Rather than us dead in the water
Reviled for our stupidity
Punished for our sins
Of appetite and flesh

He does not lecture us
Unceasingly
As bible scholars would insist

That's really who he was
In case you haven't noticed

He loved us
He still does

Oh ye ministers and holy priests

Capeesh?

THE FAITH OF THE CENTURION

Matthew 8:5–13

⁵ And when he was entered into Capernaum, there came unto him a centurion, beseeching him, ⁶ and saying, Lord, my servant lieth in the house sick of the palsy, grievously tormented. ⁷ And he saith unto him, I will come and heal him. ⁸ And the centurion answered and said, Lord, I am not worthy that thou shouldest come under my roof; but only say the word, and my servant shall be healed. ⁹ For I also am a man under authority, having under myself soldiers: and I say to this one, Go, and he goeth; and to another, Come, and he cometh; and to my servant, Do this, and he doeth it. ¹⁰ And when Jesus heard it, he marvelled, and said to them that followed, Verily I say unto you, I have not found so great faith, no, not in Israel. ¹¹ And I say unto you, that many shall come from the east and the west, and shall sit down with Abraham, and Isaac, and Jacob, in the kingdom of heaven: ¹² but the sons of the kingdom shall be cast forth into the outer darkness: there shall be the weeping and the gnashing of teeth. ¹³ And Jesus said unto the centurion, Go thy way; as thou hast believed, so be it done unto thee. And the servant was healed in that hour.

How do we heal?
Out of forgiveness of others
Especially of ourselves
Is that the deal?

At all times
We are the other
Needing only
Our forgiveness for ourselves

So consistently impossible

To prove Jesus comes from God
The tale portrays a centurion
His servant paralyzed

Only say the word and my servant will be healed

Oh yeah?

Where is this Jesus now?
In hiding?
Has he disappeared?

Where is his word
If not buried in our throats?

Everywhere lie bodies that will not heal
And physicians who no longer believe

In the present scheme of things
Science is the deity
Miraculous in the telling
Wondrous in application
Marvelous in hypothesis

Then there's us
Reaching out for something
We already possess

So say the prophets
According to the argument

Could it be faith?

REVELATION

Matthew 11:25–30

^{25} At that season Jesus answered and said, I thank thee, O Father, Lord of heaven and earth, that thou didst hide these things from the wise and understanding, and didst reveal them unto babes: ^{26} yea, Father, for so it was well-pleasing in thy sight. ^{27} All things have been delivered unto me of my Father: and no one knoweth the Son, save the Father; neither doth any know the Father, save the Son, and he to whomsoever the Son willeth to reveal him. ^{28} Come unto me, all ye that labor and are heavy laden, and I will give you rest. ^{29} Take my yoke upon you, and learn of me; for I am meek and lowly in heart: and ye shall find rest unto your souls. ^{30} For my yoke is easy, and my burden is light.

Come unto me, all ye that labor and are heavy laden
And I will give you rest

What power lies in the heart of us
We do not yet understand
Preferring to imagine
The gods look down on us
Plotting retribution
And revenge

We worship some deity
We've been taught is God
Or something close

Some kneel

Before plaster statues of the sanctified
Holinesses
Handed down
Like DNA

Jesus, Mary and Joseph
Are you deaf?
Implored the little Irish nun
Hoping they'd hear her
Straightaway

In the final analysis
Who be we
In this scheme of things
Except be slaves to anthropomorphic divinities?

If we will but
Sit quietly
Beyond the raging and the din
Beyond conflagration
And thundering
We will hear voices
In our hearts
That tell us
We are loved from all eternity

They tell us yes
We
The weary and the beaten down

Will be granted rest

Sit still

And listen carefully

JESUS RAISES A WIDOW'S SON

Luke 7:11–17

[11] *And it came to pass soon afterwards, that he went to a city called Nain; and his disciples went with him, and a great multitude.* [12] *Now when he drew near to the gate of the city, behold, there was carried out one that was dead, the only son of his mother, and she was a widow: and much people of the city was with her.* [13] *And when the Lord saw her, he had compassion on her, and said unto her, Weep not.* [14] *And he came nigh and touched the bier: and the bearers stood still. And he said, Young man, I say unto thee, Arise.* [15] *And he that was dead sat up, and began to speak. And he gave him to his mother.* [16] *And fear took hold on all: and they glorified God, saying, A great prophet is arisen among us: and, God hath visited his people.* [17] *And this report went forth concerning him in the whole of Judæa, and all the region round about.*

The dead don't cry
They listen for the go-ahead
To sit up and chatter
With the rest of us

Geniuses and fools
No doubt
Spewing stories of
Who's cheating on who
And whom
Who's pregnant
Who's running for president
Courtesy of god or shaman

Whomever
However
You please

Until once again
In the natural course of things
The dead lie down
And be gone again
We do

Once again
Awaiting resurrection
And rebirth
And further conversation
About the weather
And the latest President
Not to mention the Academy Awards

YOU HAVE NOT DANCED

Matthew 11:16–30

16 *But whereunto shall I liken this generation? It is like unto children sitting in the marketplaces, who call unto their fellows* 17 *and say, We piped unto you, and ye did not dance; we wailed, and ye did not mourn.* 18 *For John came neither eating nor drinking, and they say, He hath a demon.* 19 *The Son of man came eating and drinking, and they say, Behold, a gluttonous man and a winebibber, a friend of publicans and sinners! And wisdom is justified by her works.*

20 *Then began he to upbraid the cities wherein most of his mighty works were done, because they repented not.* 21 *Woe unto thee, Chorazin! woe unto thee, Bethsaida! for if the mighty works had been done in Tyre and Sidon which were done in you, they would have repented long ago in sackcloth and ashes.* 22 *But I say unto you, it shall be more tolerable for Tyre and Sidon in the day of judgment, than for you.* 23 *And thou, Capernaum, shalt thou be exalted unto heaven? thou shalt go down unto Hades: for if the mighty works had been done in Sodom which were done in thee, it would have remained until this day.* 24 *But I say unto you that it shall be more tolerable for the land of Sodom in the day of judgment, than for thee.*

25 *At that season Jesus answered and said, I thank thee, O Father, Lord of heaven and earth, that thou didst hide these things from the wise and understanding, and didst reveal them unto babes:* 26 *yea, Father, for so it was well-pleasing in thy sight.* 27 *All things have been delivered unto me of my Father: and no one knoweth the Son, save the Father; neither doth any know the Father, save the Son, and he to whomsoever the Son willeth to reveal him.* 28 *Come unto me, all ye that labor and are heavy laden, and I will give you rest.* 29 *Take my yoke upon*

you, and learn of me; for I am meek and lowly in heart: and ye shall find rest unto your souls. [30] *For my yoke is easy, and my burden is light.*

We piped unto you,
Ye did not dance
We wailed
Ye did not mourn

What will it take
To break
Your stillness
As you sit paralyzed
In the marketplace

With daily reports
Of massacres
Suicides
Furious opinion
And deafening despair?

A variety of remedies
Makers Mark
Jamisons
Stolichnaya
Maybe even electroshock
Make us tango
Foxtrot
Jitterbug
And generally swivel our butt
Hot cha!

This time
We did not dance
Thas right
We are loaded down with holocausts

Intimations of indigence
Pandemics
A million excuses
To be inadequate

We fail
To change ourselves
Much less transform the world

Where do we go from here
He said
She said
Except to surrender
To whom it may concern?

Come unto me, all ye that labor and are heavy laden, and I will give you rest

He said

Would that be us?

BEELZEBUB

Matthew 12:22–36

²² *Then was brought unto him one possessed with a demon, blind and dumb: and he healed him, insomuch that the dumb man spake and saw.* ²³ *And all the multitudes were amazed, and said, Can this be the son of David?* ²⁴ *But when the Pharisees heard it, they said, This man doth not cast out demons, but by Beelzebub the prince of the demons.* ²⁵ *And knowing their thoughts he said unto them, Every kingdom divided against itself is brought to desolation; and every city or house divided against itself shall not stand:* ²⁶ *and if Satan casteth out Satan, he is divided against himself; how then shall his kingdom stand?* ²⁷ *And if I by Beelzebub cast out demons, by whom do your sons cast them out? therefore shall they be your judges.* ²⁸ *But if I by the Spirit of God cast out demons, then is the kingdom of God come upon you.* ²⁹ *Or how can one enter into the house of the strong man, and spoil his goods, except he first bind the strong man? and then he will spoil his house.* ³⁰ *He that is not with me is against me; and he that gathereth not with me scattereth.* ³¹ *Therefore I say unto you, Every sin and blasphemy shall be forgiven unto men; but the blasphemy against the Spirit shall not be forgiven.* ³² *And whosoever shall speak a word against the Son of man, it shall be forgiven him; but whosoever shall speak against the Holy Spirit, it shall not be forgiven him, neither in this world, nor in that which is to come.* ³³ *Either make the tree good, and its fruit good; or make the tree corrupt, and its fruit corrupt: for the tree is known by its fruit.* ³⁴ *Ye offspring of vipers, how can ye, being evil, speak good things? for out of the abundance of the heart the mouth speaketh.* ³⁵ *The good man out of his good treasure bringeth forth good things: and the evil man out of his evil treasure bringeth forth evil things.* ³⁶ *And I say unto you, that every idle word that men shall speak, they shall give account thereof in*

the day of judgment. [37] *For by thy words thou shalt be justified, and by thy words thou shalt be condemned.*

Blasphemy against the Spirit
Shall not be forgiven

If life itself is holy
As breath is holy
And water and air come riding by

If life holds
Birth
And beauty at its core
And hears the cries of every wounded animal
And wipes the tears of those
Who have lost their own
To insurgents at every turn
One wonders what nourishes the soul

Surely some power we do not yet know
Uplifts our simple hearts
With the understanding
We are but a particle

A speck

A flash of light

Sustained by a thundering tide of worlds
A million light years away

Still
We can laugh at how ridiculous we are
And love one another
This as close as we can come to God

In which case

Why would anyone blaspheme?

JONAH

Matthew 12:38–45

³⁸ *Then certain of the scribes and Pharisees answered him, saying, Teacher, we would see a sign from thee.* ³⁹ *But he answered and said unto them, An evil and adulterous generation seeketh after a sign; and there shall no sign be given to it but the sign of Jonah the prophet:* ⁴⁰ *for as Jonah was three days and three nights in the belly of the whale; so shall the Son of man be three days and three nights in the heart of the earth.* ⁴¹ *The men of Nineveh shall stand up in the judgment with this generation, and shall condemn it: for they repented at the preaching of Jonah; and behold, a greater than Jonah is here.* ⁴² *The queen of the south shall rise up in the judgment with this generation, and shall condemn it: for she came from the ends of the earth to hear the wisdom of Solomon; and behold, a greater than Solomon is here.* ⁴³ *But the unclean spirit, when he is gone out of the man, passeth through waterless places, seeking rest, and findeth it not.* ⁴⁴ *Then he saith, I will return into my house whence I came out; and when he is come, he findeth it empty, swept, and garnished.* ⁴⁵ *Then goeth he, and taketh with himself seven other spirits more evil than himself, and they enter in and dwell there: and the last state of that man becometh worse than the first. Even so shall it be also unto this evil generation.*

Oh Jonah
He lived in dat whale

It Ain't Necessarily So

Jonah the prophet
Addressing a wicked generation

Devils occupy the best of us
Screaming obscenities
At the pure of heart

The things that we're liable
To read in the Bible
Do not necessarily
Address the overlapping
Coinciding
Truths and half-truths
Shadows in the prevailing light
Contradictions everywhere
That make us who we are

Male and female
Young and old
Celibate
Transsexual
Promiscuous
Bomb throwing
Pacifists
We are the delicious
And the damned

Perverted
Pure
Canonized
Contrarians
Protesting

All we want
Is Mom
And apple pie

Ain't that the truf?

WHO IS MY MOTHER?

Matthew 12:46–50

⁴⁶ *While he was yet speaking to the multitudes, behold, his mother and his brethren stood without, seeking to speak to him.* ⁴⁷ *And one said unto him, Behold, thy mother and thy brethren stand without, seeking to speak to thee.* ⁴⁸ *But he answered and said unto him that told him, Who is my mother? and who are my brethren?* ⁴⁹ *And he stretched forth his hand towards his disciples, and said, Behold, my mother and my brethren!* ⁵⁰ *For whosoever shall do the will of my Father who is in heaven, he is my brother, and sister, and mother.*

Who is my mother?
What about Mae West?
Maybe Marilyn Monroe?
Hello?

Fantasies supplant lost souls
Even me
No doubt

Speaking of mothers
What about Shiva?
Isis?
Anything but flesh and blood
And the rules of survival
Right?

Real or imagined
Mothers carry me
Alive and kicking
Into the womb of eternity
Where memory holds court
In the night of unknowing

Mother and brothers
It's never been good
For too many of us

Mothers looking for themselves
Backwards into infinity
Cannot embrace their sons
Seeing before them
Fathers and uncles
Emerging again
To dominate and wound

With the best of us
Comes revolution
And empowerment

With the worst
Abandonment
Into unrelenting DNA

Who can blame mothers
Except psychiatrists?

Love and affection –

Ain't that what grandmothers are for?

THE PARABLE OF THE SOWER

Matthew 13:1–23

¹ *On that day went Jesus out of the house, and sat by the sea side.* ² *And there were gathered unto him great multitudes, so that he entered into a boat, and sat; and all the multitude stood on the beach.* ³ *And he spake to them many things in parables, saying, Behold, the sower went forth to sow;* ⁴ *and as he sowed, some seeds fell by the way side, and the birds came and devoured them:* ⁵ *and others fell upon the rocky places, where they had not much earth: and straightway they sprang up, because they had no deepness of earth:* ⁶ *and when the sun was risen, they were scorched; and because they had no root, they withered away.* ⁷ *And others fell upon the thorns; and the thorns grew up and choked them:* ⁸ *and others fell upon the good ground, and yielded fruit, some a hundredfold, some sixty, some thirty.* ⁹ *He that hath ears, let him hear.*

¹⁰ *And the disciples came, and said unto him, Why speakest thou unto them in parables?* ¹¹ *And he answered and said unto them, Unto you it is given to know the mysteries of the kingdom of heaven, but to them it is not given.* ¹² *For whosoever hath, to him shall be given, and he shall have abundance: but whosoever hath not, from him shall be taken away even that which he hath.* ¹³ *Therefore speak I to them in parables; because seeing they see not, and hearing they hear not, neither do they understand.* ¹⁴ *And unto them is fulfilled the prophecy of Isaiah, which saith,*

> *By hearing ye shall hear, and shall in no wise understand;*
> *And seeing ye shall see, and shall in no wise perceive:*
> ¹⁵ *For this people's heart is waxed gross,*
> *And their ears are dull of hearing,*
> *And their eyes they have closed;*
> *Lest haply they should perceive with their eyes,*

And hear with their ears,
And understand with their heart,
And should turn again,
And I should heal them.

[16] But blessed are your eyes, for they see; and your ears, for they hear. [17] For verily I say unto you, that many prophets and righteous men desired to see the things which ye see, and saw them not; and to hear the things which ye hear, and heard them not. [18] Hear then ye the parable of the sower. [19] When any one heareth the word of the kingdom, and understandeth it not, then cometh the evil one, and snatcheth away that which hath been sown in his heart. This is he that was sown by the way side. [20] And he that was sown upon the rocky places, this is he that heareth the word, and straightway with joy receiveth it; [21] yet hath he not root in himself, but endureth for a while; and when tribulation or persecution ariseth because of the word, straightway he stumbleth. [22] And he that was sown among the thorns, this is he that heareth the word; and the care of the world, and the deceitfulness of riches, choke the word, and he becometh unfruitful. [23] And he that was sown upon the good ground, this is he that heareth the word, and understandeth it; who verily beareth fruit, and bringeth forth, some a hundredfold, some sixty, some thirty.

Seeing they see not
Hearing, they hear not
Nor do they understand

Could that be me?
Hearing nothing
But the clattering of coins
Seeing mostly
My face in the mirror
And occasional cover girls

The rustling of currency
Overrules justice

Directs armies
And ICBMs
Determines national boundaries
And the northward flow of Africans
Mexicans
And assorted refugees
Members of the ordinary human race

We see everything
Without focusing
In the mind's eye
The universe becomes a blur
Fog and desperation

Good-looking people inherit the earth
Until their teeth turn beige
And their hair evaporates

After which
Replacements carry forth
They dominate the DOW
And the dollar
Cashing in on sexual attraction
While they still have time

We come blinded by the light
Confusing it with
Strict morality
And best sellers in the New York Times

When what has been revealed
Turns out to be
The universal beating heart of love

THE PARABLE OF THE MUSTARD SEED

Matthew 13:31–35

³¹ *Another parable set he before them, saying, The kingdom of heaven is like unto a grain of mustard seed, which a man took, and sowed in his field:* ³² *which indeed is less than all seeds; but when it is grown, it is greater than the herbs, and becometh a tree, so that the birds of the heaven come and lodge in the branches thereof.*

³³ *Another parable spake he unto them; The kingdom of heaven is like unto leaven, which a woman took, and hid in three measures of meal, till it was all leavened.*

³⁴ *All these things spake Jesus in parables unto the multitudes; and without a parable spake he nothing unto them:* ³⁵ *that it might be fulfilled which was spoken through the prophet, saying,*

I will open my mouth in parables;
I will utter things hidden from the foundation of the world.

Who plants mustard seed
When you buy Gulden's at the grocery store
Or Heinz
Or order out?

Is humor inappropriate
Even with the Trinity?

As this fable goes to press
Birds will dwell in the branches
Of the mustard tree

Heaven is like that too
An Islamic tapestry
Swallows repousse
Enameled swifts
Doves with diamond eyes

Alighting on expansion
And flight
Persistent
Melodies
Silent and untraceable
That somehow reach the heart

THE PARABLE OF THE TARES

Matthew 13:36–43

³⁶ *Then he left the multitudes, and went into the house: and his disciples came unto him, saying, Explain unto us the parable of the tares of the field.* ³⁷ *And he answered and said, He that soweth the good seed is the Son of man;* ³⁸ *and the field is the world; and the good seed, these are the sons of the kingdom; and the tares are the sons of the evil one;* ³⁹ *and the enemy that sowed them is the devil: and the harvest is the end of the world; and the reapers are angels.* ⁴⁰ *As therefore the tares are gathered up and burned with fire; so shall it be in the end of the world.* ⁴¹ *The Son of man shall send forth his angels, and they shall gather out of his kingdom all things that cause stumbling, and them that do iniquity,* ⁴² *and shall cast them into the furnace of fire: there shall be the weeping and the gnashing of teeth.* ⁴³ *Then shall the righteous shine forth as the sun in the kingdom of their Father. He that hath ears, let him hear.*

Tares in the field

Angels again
This time
Harvesting enemies

There will be weeping and gnashing of teeth
According to the parable
When those who do evil
The malevolent ones
Are delivered into fire

Evildoers described as tares
Which means weeds
Imagine that

Weeds as we well know
Can be misdiagnosed
Some can flower
Some be genetically modified

Why do we need angels
When we have ourselves?

We remain subservient
To the attractive
The charming
And the rich
That's why

We need angel guardians
Pillars of thunder and fire
To burn us loose
From the Dow
That's how

Hope not
Want not
Celebrate the wonder of the earth
And the beauty of yourself

Embrace the angels
Who watch over you

Most of all

Embrace yourselves

THE PARABLE OF THE PEARL

Matthew 13:44–46

⁴⁴ *The kingdom of heaven is like unto a treasure hidden in the field; which a man found, and hid; and in his joy he goeth and selleth all that he hath, and buyeth that field.*

⁴⁵ *Again, the kingdom of heaven is like unto a man that is a merchant seeking goodly pearls:* ⁴⁶ *and having found one pearl of great price, he went and sold all that he had, and bought it.*

Buccaneers expend their lives
Investigating gold
Preoccupied with booty
Designated on a pirate map
Whispered about among thieves

Yo ho ho
And a bottle of rum
Not to mention
Methadone
Vicodin
Gilbey's Gin
And Ecstasy

Is that how we search for Heaven?
Do we require
A National Geographic entourage
A thousand shovels
And probable slaves

To find what we're looking for?

Past alcohol
And a thousand confessions
Past multiple affairs
And a team of therapists
Past doubt and despair
Past music and art

We surrender
Into unknowingness

And discover Heaven
Where we imagined
There was only night

JESUS CALMS THE STORM

Matthew 8:23–27

23 And when he was entered into a boat, his disciples followed him. 24 And behold, there arose a great tempest in the sea, insomuch that the boat was covered with the waves: but he was asleep. 25 And they came to him, and awoke him, saying, Save, Lord; we perish. 26 And he saith unto them, Why are ye fearful, O ye of little faith? Then he arose, and rebuked the winds and the sea; and there was a great calm. 27 And the men marvelled, saying, What manner of man is this, that even the winds and the sea obey him?

How do you calm a sudden storm
Rebuking winds
Resolving waves?

With good intentions
And assertive tone
Basso profundo
If possible

Did Jesus really command the squall
To cease?

He did so majestically
As the story goes
Or is that religious marketing
From Canterbury
The Vatican

And Bob Jones University?

Commanding the surf
Did not work for King Canute
Parking his throne in the oncoming tide
Ordering it to reverse itself
Until he almost drowned.

So much for royalty
In the imitation of Christ

If the story is a metaphor
Then say so
Sweet religionists

Even the likes of me
Can order a bully
To lower his voice
And put away the pistol
And the whip

They will do so immediately

Is that not so?

Ho ho

You cannot heal a man
Without touching him
More importantly
Letting him touch you

Shifting energy
And the flow of empathy

God does not heal through hate
The shaman heals
By channeling frequencies
And breathing with the world

Even witches heal
By making love to everything alive

We have no magic
Except adoration
We have no healing
Without flesh to hold
And bodies to embrace

We know that we are one

Except when our intellects
Inform us otherwise

Whom then do we listen to?

THE WORKERS ARE FEW

Matthew 9:35–38

35 And Jesus went about all the cities and the villages, teaching in their synagogues, and preaching the gospel of the kingdom, and healing all manner of disease and all manner of sickness. 36 But when he saw the multitudes, he was moved with compassion for them, because they were distressed and scattered, as sheep not having a shepherd. 37 Then saith he unto his disciples, The harvest indeed is plenteous, but the laborers are few. 38 Pray ye therefore the Lord of the harvest, that he send forth laborers into his harvest.

Have compassion on the crowds
They are yourself

College graduates
Call crowds masses
Blotting out singular souls
And facial expressions
To bolster class warfare
No doubt
As if they
In their generation
Have ever known
The meaning
Of themselves

What's wrong with you
Mr. Matthew Evangelical

Putting words in Jesus' mouth:
"Sheep without a shepherd"
Wow

Would this avatar
This prince of peace
This ikon of divinity
Liken his own
To animals?

Have compassion on the crowds
The milling throng
The mobs
The multitudes
And begin to know thyself

JESUS SENDS OUT THE TWELVE

Matthew 10:1–15

^{1} And he called unto him his twelve disciples, and gave them authority over unclean spirits, to cast them out, and to heal all manner of disease and all manner of sickness.

^{2} Now the names of the twelve apostles are these: The first, Simon, who is called Peter, and Andrew his brother; James the son of Zebedee, and John his brother; ^{3} Philip, and Bartholomew; Thomas, and Matthew the publican; James the son of Alphæus, and Thaddæus; ^{4} Simon the Cananæan, and Judas Iscariot, who also betrayed him.

^{5} These twelve Jesus sent forth, and charged them, saying, Go not into any way of the Gentiles, and enter not into any city of the Samaritans: ^{6} but go rather to the lost sheep of the house of Israel. ^{7} And as ye go, preach, saying, The kingdom of heaven is at hand. ^{8} Heal the sick, raise the dead, cleanse the lepers, cast out demons: freely ye received, freely give. ^{9} Get you no gold, nor silver, nor brass in your purses; ^{10} no wallet for your journey, neither two coats, nor shoes, nor staff: for the laborer is worthy of his food. ^{11} And into whatsoever city or village ye shall enter, search out who in it is worthy; and there abide till ye go forth. ^{12} And as ye enter into the house, salute it. ^{13} And if the house be worthy, let your peace come upon it: but if it be not worthy, let your peace return to you. ^{14} And whosoever shall not receive you, nor hear your words, as ye go forth out of that house or that city, shake off the dust of your feet. ^{15} Verily I say unto you, It shall be more tolerable for the land of Sodom and Gomorrah in the day of judgment, than for that city.

The kingdom of heaven is near
If you let it be

If you open your heart to me
And I to you
If we take down our barriers
Calling our gods
And our allegiances
By different names
And put away our guns
And our invading fears

If we look into each other's eyes
And see our souls
Staring into each other's light
And joy
Behind the barricades
We will find heaven

And if not heaven

Something better than this

Yes, we will find ourselves

AND AGAIN

Mark 6:4–13

⁴ And Jesus said unto them, A prophet is not without honor, save in his own country, and among his own kin, and in his own house. ⁵ And he could there do no mighty work, save that he laid his hands upon a few sick folk, and healed them. ⁶ And he marvelled because of their unbelief. And he went round about the villages teaching.

⁷ And he calleth unto him the twelve, and began to send them forth by two and two; and he gave them authority over the unclean spirits; ⁸ and he charged them that they should take nothing for their journey, save a staff only; no bread, no wallet, no money in their purse; ⁹ but to go shod with sandals: and, said he, put not on two coats. ¹⁰ And he said unto them, Wheresoever ye enter into a house, there abide till ye depart thence. ¹¹ And whatsoever place shall not receive you, and they hear you not, as ye go forth thence, shake off the dust that is under your feet for a testimony unto them. ¹² And they went out, and preached that men should repent. ¹³ And they cast out many demons, and anointed with oil many that were sick, and healed them.

Whatsoever place shall not receive you
And they hear you not
As ye go forth thence
Shake off the dust that is under your feet

Evil souls encircle us
They do
Even if you don't believe
They persist like viruses

Telling us we are
Nonentities

Pilgrim
Don't bother to knock

Light up the night
Attend to kinder voices
Listen for the murmuring of love

If you arrive
Announcing freedom
For everyone alive
Those who have ears to hear
As the story goes
Will welcome you
And celebrate your song

Those who have eyes
Will look into your soul
And celebrate

Believe in life as it comes to you
Or would you rather curse the dark
And the devils who dwell within?

Whatsoever place shall not receive you
Shake the dust off your feet
The shit off your shoes
Erase the untimely memory

And get the hell out of there

THE BAPTIST BEHEADED

Matthew 14:1–12

¹ At that season Herod the tetrarch heard the report concerning Jesus, ² and said unto his servants, This is John the Baptist; he is risen from the dead; and therefore do these powers work in him. ³ For Herod had laid hold on John, and bound him, and put him in prison for the sake of Herodias, his brother Philip's wife. ⁴ For John said unto him, It is not lawful for thee to have her. ⁵ And when he would have put him to death, he feared the multitude, because they counted him as a prophet. ⁶ But when Herod's birthday came, the daughter of Herodias danced in the midst, and pleased Herod. ⁷ Whereupon he promised with an oath to give her whatsoever she should ask. ⁸ And she, being put forward by her mother, saith, Give me here on a platter the head of John the Baptist. ⁹ And the king was grieved; but for the sake of his oaths, and of them that sat at meat with him, he commanded it to be given; ¹⁰ and he sent and beheaded John in the prison. ¹¹ And his head was brought on a platter, and given to the damsel: and she brought it to her mother. ¹² And his disciples came, and took up the corpse, and buried him; and they went and told Jesus.

The severed head belonged to a moralist
He went too far
Messing with the marriage of the king

Give me the head of John the Baptist
She said to the self-important potentate
That is to say
Salome the dancing star
Following instructions from her mom

179

The queen in disrepute

Surely you know *Salome*
Columbia Pictures 1953
Redhead Rita Hayworth
Removing seven veils
And then

Give me his head on a platter!
Herod cries

Such a gift!
Proclaims her mother
In Technicolor yet
Panavision
Center stage
Entertainment the rule of thumb

Does anyone remember what the Baptist said
And why he came?

Brutality is nothing new
Not then
Not now

Revenge is real enough
Obstructionists
Get it in the neck
No big surprise
Daily executions
Decapitate eternal truths

Unsolicited advice:
Never speak your mind
To ambitious empresses

If you wish to grow old
In Florida
In a first-class nursing home
Telling tales
About when you were young
And ignorant

But really
Boys

What fun is that?

JESUS FEEDS THE FIVE THOUSAND

Mark 6:30–46

^{30} And the apostles gather themselves together unto Jesus; and they told him all things, whatsoever they had done, and whatsoever they had taught. ^{31} And he saith unto them, Come ye yourselves apart into a desert place, and rest a while. For there were many coming and going, and they had no leisure so much as to eat. ^{32} And they went away in the boat to a desert place apart. ^{33} And the people saw them going, and many knew them, and they ran together there on foot from all the cities, and outwent them. ^{34} And he came forth and saw a great multitude, and he had compassion on them, because they were as sheep not having a shepherd: and he began to teach them many things. ^{35} And when the day was now far spent, his disciples came unto him, and said, The place is desert, and the day is now far spent; ^{36} send them away, that they may go into the country and villages round about, and buy themselves somewhat to eat. ^{37} But he answered and said unto them, Give ye them to eat. And they say unto him, Shall we go and buy two hundred shillings' worth of bread, and give them to eat? ^{38} And he saith unto them, How many loaves have ye? go and see. And when they knew, they say, Five, and two fishes. ^{39} And he commanded them that all should sit down by companies upon the green grass. ^{40} And they sat down in ranks, by hundreds, and by fifties. ^{41} And he took the five loaves and the two fishes, and looking up to heaven, he blessed, and brake the loaves; and he gave to the disciples to set before them; and the two fishes divided he among them all. ^{42} And they all ate, and were filled. ^{43} And they took up broken pieces, twelve basketfuls, and also of the fishes. ^{44} And they that ate the loaves were five thousand men.

^{45} And straightway he constrained his disciples to enter into the boat, and to go before him unto the other side to Bethsaida,

---

Five loaves and two fishes
Fed five thousand folk
What's that supposed to mean?

What were they looking for
Aside from lunch?

Do we question stories
Of faith
Or do we just believe?

Whatever happened to metaphors?

Disciples do starve to death
Depending on rainfall
Climate change
Infestations
And the price of food

The Great Hunger in Eire
Reduced devotees to skeletons
Screaming
Jesus
Mary
And Joseph
As they dissolved
Into the waiting arms of death

Faith and begorrah
Cried Mother McCree

What are we to make of miracles
Tall tales
Of a god-man
Walking on water
And multiplying loaves of bread?

Or was this story merely a reminder
Of the powers that are given to us?

To feed the hungry

And pour out our hearts

If only we would

JESUS WALKS ON THE WATER

John 6:16–21

16 And when evening came, his disciples went down unto the sea; 17 and they entered into a boat, and were going over the sea unto Capernaum. And it was now dark, and Jesus had not yet come to them. 18 And the sea was rising by reason of a great wind that blew. 19 When therefore they had rowed about five and twenty or thirty furlongs, they behold Jesus walking on the sea, and drawing nigh unto the boat: and they were afraid. 20 But he saith unto them, It is I; be not afraid. 21 They were willing therefore to receive him into the boat: and straight-way the boat was at the land whither they were going.

How do you walk on water?
How do you heal the sick?
Surely there's a trick
To being God

What about restoring limbs
Reversing ALS
Dementia
Parkinsons
Or is that up to us?
Apparently so

How do you walk on water?
Carefully
Said the comedian

Probably Jesus said so too
Being God
At least according to his devotionists
He certainly loved a joke
Or at least
A vaudeville turn
What else was he here for?
Except to lighten the load
And make us laugh

And in the darkness
See the suffering of humankind

The proof of divinity
According to him
Is how you click
With the dispossessed
The homeless
The destitute
The mad

All those who are burdened
And weary of heart
Are embraced
If they will
At the center of love

And certainly

Applause

JESUS THE BREAD OF LIFE

John 6:22–40

²² *On the morrow the multitude that stood on the other side of the sea saw that there was no other boat there, save one, and that Jesus entered not with his disciples into the boat, but that his disciples went away alone* ²³ *(howbeit there came boats from Tiberias nigh unto the place where they ate the bread after the Lord had given thanks):* ²⁴ *when the multitude therefore saw that Jesus was not there, neither his disciples, they themselves got into the boats, and came to Capernaum, seeking Jesus.* ²⁵ *And when they found him on the other side of the sea, they said unto him, Rabbi, when camest thou hither?* ²⁶ *Jesus answered them and said, Verily, verily, I say unto you, Ye seek me, not because ye saw signs, but because ye ate of the loaves, and were filled.* ²⁷ *Work not for the food which perisheth, but for the food which abideth unto eternal life, which the Son of man shall give unto you: for him the Father, even God, hath sealed.* ²⁸ *They said therefore unto him, What must we do, that we may work the works of God?* ²⁹ *Jesus answered and said unto them, This is the work of God, that ye believe on him whom he hath sent.* ³⁰ *They said therefore unto him, What then doest thou for a sign, that we may see, and believe thee? what workest thou?* ³¹ *Our fathers ate the manna in the wilderness; as it is written, He gave them bread out of heaven to eat.* ³² *Jesus therefore said unto them, Verily, verily, I say unto you, It was not Moses that gave you the bread out of heaven; but my Father giveth you the true bread out of heaven.* ³³ *For the bread of God is that which cometh down out of heaven, and giveth life unto the world.* ³⁴ *They said therefore unto him, Lord, evermore give us this bread.* ³⁵ *Jesus said unto them, I am the bread of life: he that cometh to me shall not hunger, and he that believeth on me shall never thirst.* ³⁶ *But I said unto you, that ye have seen me, and yet believe not.* ³⁷ *All that which the Father giveth me shall*

come unto me; and him that cometh to me I will in no wise cast out. ³⁸ *For I am come down from heaven, not to do mine own will, but the will of him that sent me.* ³⁹ *And this is the will of him that sent me, that of all that which he hath given me I should lose nothing, but should raise it up at the last day.* ⁴⁰ *For this is the will of my Father, that every one that beholdeth the Son, and believeth on him, should have eternal life; and I will raise him up at the last day.*

One minute
Man does not live by bread alone
The next
I am the bread of life

We are drowning in metaphor
Starving for unconditional love

All the time it's sitting there
In front of us

According to the evangelicals
When we surrender to Jesus
We will no longer be overwhelmed
By alcohol
Opioids
Our neighbor's husband
Or wife
Or more importantly
The lies
We tell ourselves

With our flesh-destroying wars
We devour each other
In our hunger
For dominance

Over the riches of the land
And sea
We eviscerate the earth

When we are defeated
Encaged
Humiliated
Starved
As we will surely be
What will
The carpenter from Nazareth
Say then?

My flesh is meat indeed

Will we be cannibals
Anon
Carnivores
Encased in light?

I am the living bread come down from heaven

He says again

After two million years of skirmishes
Falling down and rising up
We are starving for a world we do not understand

And a God

We do not know

THE FAITH OF A CANAANITE WOMAN

Matthew 15:21–28

21 And Jesus went out thence, and withdrew into the parts of Tyre and Sidon. 22 And behold, a Canaanitish woman came out from those borders, and cried, saying, Have mercy on me, O Lord, thou son of David; my daughter is grievously vexed with a demon. 23 But he answered her not a word. And his disciples came and besought him, saying, Send her away; for she crieth after us. 24 But he answered and said, I was not sent but unto the lost sheep of the house of Israel. 25 But she came and worshipped him, saying, Lord, help me. 26 And he answered and said, It is not meet to take the children's bread and cast it to the dogs. 27 But she said, Yea, Lord: for even the dogs eat of the crumbs which fall from their masters' table. 28 Then Jesus answered and said unto her, O woman, great is thy faith: be it done unto thee even as thou wilt. And her daughter was healed from that hour.

We are dogs at the master's table
Waiting for crumbs
And knuckle bones

Demons possess us
Darkness overwhelms
We cry for deliverance
Hoping for release
And recompense

Expecting divine intervention
At every turn

The question looms:
Who do we think we are?
Who have we ever been?

Do we believe
Claims of divinity
Of sky gods
Arising
Resurrecting
Assumed into heaven
A patriarchal deity or two in every tribe
Claiming they love us
And will return one day

We are told
Despair denotes the baddest sin
Against the Holy Ghost

Oh good

Where do we meet in the middle?

When do we know the truth?

THE DEMAND FOR A SIGN

Matthew 16:1–4

¹ *And the Pharisees and Sadducees came, and trying him asked him to show them a sign from heaven.* ² *But he answered and said unto them, When it is evening, ye say, It will be fair weather: for the heaven is red.* ³ *And in the morning, It will be foul weather to-day: for the heaven is red and lowering. Ye know how to discern the face of the heaven; but ye cannot discern the signs of the times.* ⁴ *An evil and adulterous generation seeketh after a sign; and there shall no sign be given unto it, but the sign of Jonah. And he left them, and departed.*

Give us a sign
Said the Pharisees

Do you blame them?
They were the legalists
Some say the hypocrites
Hard to know the bottom line
When everyone is
Naming names

He said he came from heaven
Are they not entitled to a test?
He called them wicked and adulterous
Whatever that might mean
Depending on your politics

The King of Peace

As this version goes
Sounds like an evangelical
Populist
Puritanical
Scourge

Who made this up?
Who wrote it down?
When do we get to answer back?

Matthew
Mark
Luke
And John
What's with you guys?

Ye cannot discern the sign of the times

He said

Was there ever a time without storms
And battlefields
Littered with the rotting dead?

Was there ever a place
When the sky was not red and lowering?

We are delivered into lunacy
Armies tramping
Tyrants run amok
Psychopaths at every turn

The only sign of heaven
Remains the human cry for love

In the face of which
He says

Even sinners love those who love them back

Even in the best of times
There's no way out
From the relentless truth of questioning

And the fire

Of the Creator God

THE JEWS

John 7:1

¹ *And after these things Jesus walked in Galilee: for he would not walk in Judæa, because the Jews sought to kill him.*

The Jews sought to kill him

Once again
And apparently forevermore

Why are we here again

And once again?

Everyone person in this history
Of claims and anecdotes
Was Jewish
No?

You know him
Him whom they called
The King of the Jews

Some jargon
Makes you question
Everything

The gospels

May sometimes be the word of God
They are also
The words of men
And malcontents

Have faith

That means
At all times

Be wary
Of the human race

SIN NO MORE

John 8:8–11

He that is without sin
Let him cast the first stone

Capital advice

Obviously
Several hundred million
Stoners
Are following directions well

Pure souls they be
Wrecking reputations
Ruining careers
Destroying any woman
Who sticks her head
Above water
Or is it between the sheets
Too many times

To count?

Who's counting?

If you can't find a stone
Use a brick
Baseball bats are always good
What about social media?
That works

Don't let any girl you know
Get too far out of line

Go and sin no more

What is forgiveness
Except the letting go of violence
And the baggage of tears

She had three husbands
Is that a sin?
Who made these rules?
A woman condemned for falling in love again
Again
And once again

No stories about the men
She knew

One can only imagine

BLIND FROM BIRTH

John 9:1–11

¹ And as he passed by, he saw a man blind from his birth. ² And his disciples asked him, saying, Rabbi, who sinned, this man, or his parents, that he should be born blind? ³ Jesus answered, Neither did this man sin, nor his parents: but that the works of God should be made manifest in him. ⁴ We must work the works of him that sent me, while it is day: the night cometh, when no man can work. ⁵ When I am in the world, I am the light of the world. ⁶ When he had thus spoken, he spat on the ground, and made clay of the spittle, and anointed his eyes with the clay, ⁷ and said unto him, Go, wash in the pool of Siloam (which is by interpretation, Sent). He went away therefore, and washed, and came seeing. ⁸ The neighbors therefore, and they that saw him aforetime, that he was a beggar, said, Is not this he that sat and begged? ⁹ Others said, It is he: others said, No, but he is like him. He said, I am he. ¹⁰ They said therefore unto him, How then were thine eyes opened? ¹¹ He answered, The man that is called Jesus made clay, and anointed mine eyes, and said unto me, Go to Siloam, and wash: so I went away and washed, and I received sight.

We are all born blind
Bathed in black light
Sometimes
We see shadows
And flashing fire
And listen to laughter
Echoing

In the meantime

We navigate through night
And ruminate on nothingness
And doom

You open the eyes
Of those born blind
That we may see

Rubbing our eyes
In clay
Pushing us into primal mud
Until one fine day
We burst forth
Into a kaleidoscope
Of color
And in our yammering
Create a symphony

THE TRANSFIGURATION

Matthew 17:1–13

¹ And after six days Jesus taketh with him Peter, and James, and John his brother, and bringeth them up into a high mountain apart: ² and he was transfigured before them; and his face did shine as the sun, and his garments became white as the light. ³ And behold, there appeared unto them Moses and Elijah talking with him. ⁴ And Peter answered, and said unto Jesus, Lord, it is good for us to be here: if thou wilt, I will make here three tabernacles; one for thee, and one for Moses, and one for Elijah. ⁵ While he was yet speaking, behold, a bright cloud overshadowed them: and behold, a voice out of the cloud, saying, This is my beloved Son, in whom I am well pleased; hear ye him. ⁶ And when the disciples heard it, they fell on their face, and were sore afraid. ⁷ And Jesus came and touched them and said, Arise, and be not afraid. ⁸ And lifting up their eyes, they saw no one, save Jesus only.

⁹ And as they were coming down from the mountain, Jesus commanded them, saying, Tell the vision to no man, until the Son of man be risen from the dead. ¹⁰ And his disciples asked him, saying, Why then say the scribes that Elijah must first come? ¹¹ And he answered and said, Elijah indeed cometh, and shall restore all things: ¹² but I say unto you, that Elijah is come already, and they knew him not, but did unto him whatsoever they would. Even so shall the Son of man also suffer of them. ¹³ Then understood the disciples that he spake unto them of John the Baptist.

Under sleep
And incandescent flame
The soul eternal

Blazes forth

Jesus in the spotlight
Mr. Moses
And Elijah
Standing by

Baby, you'd better believe

Will we be transfigured too?
On a mountaintop
Looking down on Earth
Where we belong

Things are never what they seem
The leitmotif of Christendom

The dead come rushing in
Prophets reappear
Surprise

Once
You either believed
Or not
In which case
The Inquisition would have had your head
At the very least
Taken your portfolio
Maybe even repossessed
Your Chevrolet

The Transfiguration:
Theatre of the Ridiculous
Is that not so?

Let us build temples to light shows
And the blaze of atom bombs

What, no Nebuchadnezzar?
How about the Holy Ghost?
No doubt a dove on a guywire
How about Adam and Eve?
In case you don't believe in Bethlehem

Divinity unwrapped
Vegas on the mountaintop
Strobe lights flashing
Standing room only
Take it on the road

Children
Now do you believe?

What was the aftermath?
Did Transfiguration
Transform the pain to come
And the grief
Of humankind in shards
Our souls a feeding ground for sharks?

What does the Transfiguration
Have to do
With us?

THE DEATH OF LAZARUS

John 11:1–36

¹ Now a certain man was sick, Lazarus of Bethany, of the village of Mary and her sister Martha. ² And it was that Mary who anointed the Lord with ointment, and wiped his feet with her hair, whose brother Lazarus was sick. ³ The sisters therefore sent unto him, saying, Lord, behold, he whom thou lovest is sick. ⁴ But when Jesus heard it, he said, This sickness is not unto death, but for the glory of God, that the Son of God may be glorified thereby. ⁵ Now Jesus loved Martha, and her sister, and Lazarus. ⁶ When therefore he heard that he was sick, he abode at that time two days in the place where he was. ⁷ Then after this he saith to the disciples, Let us go into Judæa again. ⁸ The disciples say unto him, Rabbi, the Jews were but now seeking to stone thee; and goest thou thither again? ⁹ Jesus answered, Are there not twelve hours in the day? If a man walk in the day, he stumbleth not, because he seeth the light of this world. ¹⁰ But if a man walk in the night, he stumbleth, because the light is not in him. ¹¹ These things spake he: and after this he saith unto them, Our friend Lazarus is fallen asleep; but I go, that I may awake him out of sleep. ¹² The disciples therefore said unto him, Lord, if he is fallen asleep, he will recover. ¹³ Now Jesus had spoken of his death: but they thought that he spake of taking rest in sleep. ¹⁴ Then Jesus therefore said unto them plainly, Lazarus is dead. ¹⁵ And I am glad for your sakes that I was not there, to the intent ye may believe; nevertheless let us go unto him. ¹⁶ Thomas therefore, who is called Didymus, said unto his fellow-disciples, Let us also go, that we may die with him.

¹⁷ So when Jesus came, he found that he had been in the tomb four days already. ¹⁸ Now Bethany was nigh unto Jerusalem, about fifteen furlongs off; ¹⁹ and many of the Jews had come to Martha and Mary, to console them concerning their brother. ²⁰ Martha therefore, when she heard that Jesus was coming, went and met him: but Mary still sat in the house. ²¹ *Martha therefore said unto Jesus, Lord, if thou hadst been here, my brother had not died.* ²² *And even now I know that, whatsoever thou shalt ask of God, God will give thee.* ²³ *Jesus saith unto her, Thy brother shall rise again.* ²⁴ *Martha saith unto him, I know that he shall rise again in the resurrection at the last day.* ²⁵ *Jesus said unto her, I am the resurrection, and the life: he that believeth on me, though he die, yet shall he live;* ²⁶ *and whosoever liveth and believeth on me shall never die. Believest thou this?* ²⁷ *She saith unto him, Yea, Lord: I have believed that thou art the Christ, the Son of God, even he that cometh into the world.* ²⁸ *And when she had said this, she went away, and called Mary her sister secretly, saying, The Teacher is here, and calleth thee.* ²⁹ *And she, when she heard it, arose quickly, and went unto him.* ³⁰ *(Now Jesus was not yet come into the village, but was still in the place where Martha met him.)* ³¹ *The Jews then who were with her in the house, and were consoling her, when they saw Mary, that she rose up quickly and went out, followed her, supposing that she was going unto the tomb to weep there.* ³² *Mary therefore, when she came where Jesus was, and saw him, fell down at his feet, saying unto him, Lord, if thou hadst been here, my brother had not died.* ³³ *When Jesus therefore saw her weeping, and the Jews also weeping who came with her, he groaned in the spirit, and was troubled,* ³⁴ *and said, Where have ye laid him? They say unto him, Lord, come and see.* ³⁵ *Jesus wept.* ³⁶ *The Jews therefore said, Behold how he loved him!*

Lazarus
A longtime friend
Bit the dust one day

And Jesus wept

This is proof of holiness?
If so
We are being played

As the story goes
Jesus raised him from the dead
To prove
He's God
Apparently

Compassion
Forgiveness
Unconditional love for his enemies
All signs of the Nazarene
Doesn't quite do it

What else you need to know?

Does the rabbi in question
Need to raise the dead
Walk on water
Multiply the loaves
In effect
Produce a magic show
To demonstrate divinity?

In which case
Houdini was also God

How is the good news of salvation
So-called
Any different from the ordinary life?

We are born
We fall in love
We reproduce
Sometimes we go to war
We die
Sometimes we learn to read

Make shoefly pie
Barbecue
And sometimes sing

These are our parameters

And Jesus wept

Do we remember anything else?
In short order
Lazarus died a second time
And Jesus did as well
You might recall

And so will you

Who weeps for the rest of us?

From the beginning
Until the end
And afterwards

Our tears flow like rivers
Into the ocean of remembering

Perhaps laughter
Is the greater proof
Of God

MARTHA, MARTHA

Luke 10:38–42

³⁸ *Now as they went on their way, he entered into a certain village: and a certain woman named Martha received him into her house.* ³⁹ *And she had a sister called Mary, who also sat at the Lord's feet, and heard his word.* ⁴⁰ *But Martha was cumbered about much serving; and she came up to him, and said, Lord, dost thou not care that my sister did leave me to serve alone? bid her therefore that she help me.* ⁴¹ *But the Lord answered and said unto her, Martha, Martha, thou art anxious and troubled about many things:* ⁴² *but one thing is needful: for Mary hath chosen the good part, which shall not be taken away from her.*

Martha Martha

Hail to the saints of the commonplace
They bake the bread
Scramble the eggs
Wash the diapers
Scrub the floors
Listen to the longwinded and the weary
The catalogue is long

Martha Martha
Have you no secrets?
No shadows?
Are you merely a lyric in our midst?

The good woman
The faithful friend

Did this visitor not make claims
About a virgin birth
An immaculate conception
Magi hovering

Did he share with you
He was the Second Person of the Blessed Trinity
The Alpha and the Omega?
Well?

Or did the next generation of devotees
After you
Come up with that conceit?

The idea of a backcountry carpenter
Did someone say rabbi
Suddenly become the Son of God
What did you think?
What did you say?

He paid attention to the least of us
The unloved
The dispossessed
The wounded us

Was that not proof of divinity enough?

Or was he just another vagabond
Spouting platitudes?

Love your neighbor as yourself

Was that the gist of it?

Did you ever wonder why he came to you?

Why?

To say you are anxious and troubled
About many things, too many things
No doubt
That your sister was some kind of mystic
When all she did was lie around
And worship him?

While you cleaned the house
Cooked the meals
And made everything that followed
Possible?

You'd have to wonder

Wouldn't you?

MARY THE MAGDALEN

Luke 7:36–50

36 *And one of the Pharisees desired him that he would eat with him. And he entered into the Pharisee's house, and sat down to meat.* 37 *And behold, a woman who was in the city, a sinner; and when she knew that he was sitting at meat in the Pharisee's house, she brought an alabaster cruse of ointment,* 38 *and standing behind at his feet, weeping, she began to wet his feet with her tears, and wiped them with the hair of her head, and kissed his feet, and anointed them with the ointment.* 39 *Now when the Pharisee that had bidden him saw it, he spake within himself, saying, This man, if he were a prophet, would have perceived who and what manner of woman this is that toucheth him, that she is a sinner.* 40 *And Jesus answering said unto him, Simon, I have somewhat to say unto thee. And he saith, Teacher, say on.* 41 *A certain lender had two debtors: the one owed five hundred shillings, and the other fifty.* 42 *When they had not wherewith to pay, he forgave them both. Which of them therefore will love him most?* 43 *Simon answered and said, He, I suppose, to whom he forgave the most. And he said unto him, Thou hast rightly judged.* 44 *And turning to the woman, he said unto Simon, Seest thou this woman? I entered into thy house, thou gavest me no water for my feet: but she hath wetted my feet with her tears, and wiped them with her hair.* 45 *Thou gavest me no kiss: but she, since the time I came in, hath not ceased to kiss my feet.* 46 *My head with oil thou didst not anoint: but she hath anointed my feet with ointment.* 47 *Wherefore I say unto thee, Her sins, which are many, are forgiven; for she loved much: but to whom little is forgiven, the same loveth little.* 48 *And he said unto her, Thy sins are forgiven.* 49 *And they that sat at meat with him began to say within themselves, Who is this that even forgiveth sins?* 50 *And he said unto the woman, Thy faith hath saved thee; go in peace.*

Luke 8:1–2

1 And it came to pass soon afterwards, that he went about through cities and villages, preaching and bringing the good tidings of the kingdom of God, and with him the twelve, 2 and certain women who had been healed of evil spirits and infirmities: Mary that was called Magdalene, from whom seven demons had gone out.

Mary Mary
Maria
Marie
Who are you now?

Stories of you
Whoever you are
Or used to be
Abound

Were you Martha's sister
Sitting by your master's feet

Or Mary
Out of whom seven devils were gone forth?

Or the sinner
With the alabaster box?

Will we ever know?

One scholar calls you a proprietor
Another a prostitute
Another a spiritual devotee
Too many Maries to count

Were you but a reference point?
The source of unending argument
Were you a prop for an anecdote?
Or the center of the big reveal?

Where you a who
Or a ho
Or a buttoned-down MBA?

Inquiring minds
Still want to know
In what land
Do ordinary women
Presumably respectable
Pour perfume on a gentleman?

JESUS RAISES LAZARUS FROM THE DEAD

John 11:38–47

38 Jesus therefore again groaning in himself cometh to the tomb. Now it was a cave, and a stone lay against it. 39 Jesus saith, Take ye away the stone. Martha, the sister of him that was dead, saith unto him, Lord, by this time the body decayeth; for he hath been dead four days. 40 Jesus saith unto her, Said I not unto thee, that, if thou believedst, thou shouldest see the glory of God? 41 So they took away the stone. And Jesus lifted up his eyes, and said, Father, I thank thee that thou heardest me. 42 And I knew that thou hearest me always: but because of the multitude that standeth around I said it, that they may believe that thou didst send me. 43 And when he had thus spoken, he cried with a loud voice, Lazarus, come forth. 44 He that was dead came forth, bound hand and foot with grave-clothes; and his face was bound about with a napkin. Jesus saith unto them, Loose him, and let him go.

45 Many therefore of the Jews, who came to Mary and beheld that which he did, believed on him. 46 But some of them went away to the Pharisees, and told them the things which Jesus had done.

He plans to rise
From the dead
He says

And so are we
If we believe in him
He says again

What if we don't believe?

Lazarus come forth

Maybe Lazarus wasn't dead
To begin with

Maybe this was staged

If you believe in me

You will rise again

Guess what Lord
We're not even sure
You rose again

Lazarus come forth

Lazarus
Whatever else
We need to chat with you

Somewhere
Between dogma
And heresy

Between subtext
And religious mania

On the other side of fantasy

Lies resurrection
And rebirth

For those of us

Who need to believe

More than anything

These days

THE POOR

John 12:1–8

¹ *Jesus therefore six days before the passover came to Bethany, where Lazarus was, whom Jesus raised from the dead.* ² *So they made him a supper there: and Martha served; but Lazarus was one of them that sat at meat with him.* ³ *Mary therefore took a pound of ointment of pure nard, very precious, and anointed the feet of Jesus, and wiped his feet with her hair: and the house was filled with the odor of the ointment.* ⁴ *But Judas Iscariot, one of his disciples, that should betray him, saith,* ⁵ *Why was not this ointment sold for three hundred shillings, and given to the poor?* ⁶ *Now this he said, not because he cared for the poor; but because he was a thief, and having the bag took away what was put therein.* ⁷ *Jesus therefore said, Suffer her to keep it against the day of my burying.* ⁸ *For the poor ye have always with you; but me ye have not always.*

For the poor you have always with you
But me you have not always

My grandfather used that line
Straight from the mouth of the sanctified
An apparent explanation
To take little notice of the poor

They're looking for a handout
A giveaway
He said

Not attractive folk in any case

217

My grandmother chimed in
Most of them are foreigners
Achtung

Who looks a homeless person
In the face?
Too uncomfortable to contemplate

I will be with you until the time of time

Who's talking here?

For the poor you have always with you
But me you have not always

That means put your money
In the collection plate

Your insurance for immortality

Apparently
I missed the point

Good thing

THE LIGHT

John 12:34–43

[34] *The multitude therefore answered him, We have heard out of the law that the Christ abideth for ever: and how sayest thou, The Son of man must be lifted up? who is this Son of man?* [35] *Jesus therefore said unto them, Yet a little while is the light among you. Walk while ye have the light, that darkness overtake you not: and he that walketh in the darkness knoweth not whither he goeth.* [36] *While ye have the light, believe on the light, that ye may become sons of light.*

These things spake Jesus, and he departed and hid himself from them. [37] *But though he had done so many signs before them, yet they believed not on him:* [38] *that the word of Isaiah the prophet might be fulfilled, which he spake,*

Lord, who hath believed our report?

And to whom hath the arm of the Lord been revealed?

[39] *For this cause they could not believe, for that Isaiah said again,*

[40] *He hath blinded their eyes, and he hardened their heart;*

Lest they should see with their eyes, and perceive with their heart,

And should turn,

And I should heal them.

[41] *These things said Isaiah, because he saw his glory; and he spake of him.* [42] *Nevertheless even of the rulers many believed on him; but because of the Pharisees they did not confess it, lest they should be put out of the synagogue:* [43] *for they loved the glory that is of men more than the glory that is of God.*

Believe on the light
That ye may become the sons of light

219

What is light to us?
The sun
The moon
The stars
A billion galaxies
Big Bang

Out of light is borne everything alive

Lasers
Floodlights
Flashlights
Halogen
Kleig lights
Strobe
Gas lights
Spotlights
Limelight
Torches
Explosions
Sunshine
Rainbows
X-rays
Candlelight
Chandeliers
Night lights
Campfires
Photography
The Internet

No

He's talking about the light in our eyes
Streaming directly from our souls

If we would only look
Into one another's eyes
And not be terrified
Behold

We would see the history of the universe
And watch the world unfold

JOHN

John 13:23–24

²³ There was at the table reclining in Jesus' bosom one of his disciples, whom Jesus loved. ²⁴ Simon Peter therefore beckoneth to him, and saith unto him, Tell us who it is of whom he speaketh.

Who is this disciple
Anonymous even then?
Knocking back the wine no doubt

Reclining on say what?

Envision
This scene at Rotary
The Knights of Columbus
The Sons of the Confederacy

Men's clubs only go so far

This is my body
Take ye and eat

The inference being what?

Clearly code
For something sacrificial

Or worse

This is my blood
Take ye and drink

Again, he went on
Upping the ante

Really?

Homophobic
Psychotic
Or a Madison Avenue
Advertising campaign?

Words fail

The imagination reels

It gets your attention
Nevertheless

Reclining on his bosom

Please

A NEW COMMANDMENT

John 14:1

[1] *Let not your heart be troubled: believe in God, believe also in me.*

Let not your heart be troubled

We of this fragile human reckoning
Anxious about ourselves
So rarely recognized
And seldom understood

Until some clergyman
A prophet of rampaging good news
Blurts out in happy tones

Let not your heart be troubled

Please contribute
To our capital campaign

Let not your heart be troubled

Turn off the news
Order a lobotomy
Cancel your suicide

Why should we care
If we are impotent

Duped
Confined
Or
Heading towards divorce?

Let not your heart be troubled

If you let yourself
Stop
In the middle of traffic
Steady yourself

You are the center of your own universe

The presence within you
Has overcome the world
He will again
If you would only stop
And consider who you are

Got that?

Good

Or good enough

THE PARACLETE

John 14:16–17

16 And I will pray the Father, and he shall give you another Comforter, that he may be with you for ever, 17 even the Spirit of truth: whom the world cannot receive; for it beholdeth him not, neither knoweth him: ye know him; for he abideth with you, and shall be in you.

He shall give you another paraclete

The comforter
The advocate
The dove
Hello?

Another metaphor
Almost too improbable to grasp

The man in the pulpit
Prates on about the paraclete
As we sit in pews
Dreaming of a river cruise and cocktails
Overlooking the Bosphorus
Wondering about orgies
Naked friends aroused
Awaiting
Flesh and fantasy

Where am I?

Who is this Holy Ghost?
Sounds like a poltergeist

The way
The life
And the truth
Bespeaks the company within
When we get around to it

And begin to understand
Exactly who we are

THE COMFORTER

John 14:24–26

24 He that loveth me not keepeth not my words: and the word which ye hear is not mine, but the Father's who sent me.

25 These things have I spoken unto you, while yet abiding with you. 26 But the Comforter, even the Holy Spirit, whom the Father will send in my name, he shall teach you all things, and bring to your remembrance all that I said unto you.

Children
Listen up
The Holy Ghost
Has changed his name
Or hers
Its Holy Spirit now

Spirit
Spiritus
Silent behind the soul

Ghosts
On the other hand
Geists to many
Are sometimes visible
Born in the forests of the night

If you stay awake
Be still
In the surrounding dim

You may come across
A phantom bright
And whispering

Begone with ghosts
The church declares
They come with Halloween

Accept the Spirit
He has sent

Drown in ecstasy
And learn to know
The fire within

Past geists
And comforters
Beyond advocates
And paracletes
And the occasional dove
With a broken wing

It all comes down to
Love

A cliché to those
Who know differently

And altogether

Otherwise

In the meantime

What about you?

JESUS HEALS TEN MEN WITH LEPROSY

Luke 17:11–19

^{11} *And it came to pass, as they were on the way to Jerusalem, that he was passing along the borders of Samaria and Galilee.* ^{12} *And as he entered into a certain village, there met him ten men that were lepers, who stood afar off:* ^{13} *and they lifted up their voices, saying, Jesus, Master, have mercy on us.* ^{14} *And when he saw them, he said unto them, Go and show yourselves unto the priests. And it came to pass, as they went, they were cleansed.* ^{15} *And one of them, when he saw that he was healed, turned back, with a loud voice glorifying God;* ^{16} *and he fell upon his face at his feet, giving him thanks: and he was a Samaritan.* ^{17} *And Jesus answering said, Were not the ten cleansed? but where are the nine?* ^{18} *Were there none found that returned to give glory to God, save this stranger?* ^{19} *And he said unto him, Arise, and go thy way: thy faith hath made thee whole.*

Here's a tale:
Ten men with leprosy
Missing body parts
And flesh
A scene too terrible to contemplate

With but a word
Jesus healed all ten
Shazam!

One came to thank him

Where are the other nine?
Jesus asked

Ain't that the truth?

Jesus
Don't be so sensitive
Advised the therapist
Why do you care?
One in ten's a pretty good ratio
Considering

You should be pleased with yourself
How many people can heal the sick?

But where are the other nine?
He said a second time

The gentleman
Who thanked him
Suddenly had a face again
Imagine that
And fingers

He thought maybe
He could write his autobiography

In fact
He said
I could bring you lots more lepers
And charge you
Maybe ten percent apiece
How's that?

This is about the presence
Of light
Said the Master

The coming of the kingdom of God

Wow
Said the leper would-have-been

Look at my new fingernails!

SUFFER THE LITTLE CHILDREN

Matthew 19:13–14

13 Then were there brought unto him little children, that he should lay his hands on them, and pray: and the disciples rebuked them. 14 But Jesus said, Suffer the little children, and forbid them not, to come unto me: for to such belongeth the kingdom of heaven.

Suffer the little children to come unto me
And forbid them not to come unto me:
For to such belongeth the kingdom of God

What's a child to do
With Jesus Christ?

Their minds not yet socialized
Jesus no different to him
Or her
Than *Here Comes Peter Cottontail*
And Santa Claus

Fundamentalists don't appreciate
Religion is hard enough
Even in the best of times

For people trained to contemplate
It's even worse

Striving to surrender

Into unconditional love
At all times
Letting the breath
Of all creation
Breathe through us

Intelligent people not likely
To fall headlong
Into the sentiments of a greeting card

Give me the child for the first seven years
I will give you the man

Said St. Ignatius Loyola
Founder of the Jesuits

By reputation and design
Wonderful people
Jesuits
Who might tend to overdo it
Especially with a six-year old

Evangelicals
However exceptional
Can become
Much too resolute

What's a child to do?

Suffer the little children
To come to the carnival
And the beach

Come to puppies
Come play

Come make fudge with me
Make masks
Jump rope
Let's go fish

That's more like it

Ever you please

THE COMING OF THE KINGDOM

Luke 17:20–37

²⁰ *And being asked by the Pharisees, when the kingdom of God cometh, he answered them and said, The kingdom of God cometh not with observation:* ²¹ *neither shall they say, Lo, here! or, There! for lo, the kingdom of God is within you.*

²² *And he said unto the disciples, The days will come, when ye shall desire to see one of the days of the Son of man, and ye shall not see it.* ²³ *And they shall say to you, Lo, there! Lo, here! go not away, nor follow after them:* ²⁴ *for as the lightning, when it lighteneth out of the one part under the heaven, shineth unto the other part under heaven; so shall the Son of man be in his day.* ²⁵ *But first must he suffer many things and be rejected of this generation.* ²⁶ *And as it came to pass in the days of Noah, even so shall it be also in the days of the Son of man.* ²⁷ *They ate, they drank, they married, they were given in marriage, until the day that Noah entered into the ark, and the flood came, and destroyed them all.* ²⁸ *Likewise even as it came to pass in the days of Lot; they ate, they drank, they bought, they sold, they planted, they builded;* ²⁹ *but in the day that Lot went out from Sodom it rained fire and brimstone from heaven, and destroyed them all:* ³⁰ *after the same manner shall it be in the day that the Son of man is revealed.* ³¹ *In that day, he that shall be on the housetop, and his goods in the house, let him not go down to take them away: and let him that is in the field likewise not return back.* ³² *Remember Lot's wife.* ³³ *Whosoever shall seek to gain his life shall lose it: but whosoever shall lose his life shall preserve it.* ³⁴ *I say unto you, In that night there shall be two men on one bed; the one shall be taken, and the other shall be left.* ³⁵ *There shall be two women grinding together; the one shall be taken, and the other shall be left.* ³⁶

²² And he said unto the disciples, The days will come, when ye shall desire to see one of the days of the Son of man, and ye shall not see it. ²³ And they shall say to you, Lo, there! Lo, here! go not away, nor follow after them: ²⁴ for as the lightning, when it lighteneth out of the one part under the heaven, shineth unto the other part under heaven; so shall the Son of man be in his day. ²⁵ But first must he suffer many things and be rejected of this generation. ²⁶ And as it came to pass in the days of Noah, even so shall it be also in the days of the Son of man. ²⁷ They ate, they drank, they married, they were given in marriage, until the day that Noah entered into the ark, and the flood came, and destroyed them all. ²⁸ Likewise even as it came to pass in the days of Lot; they ate, they drank, they bought, they sold, they planted, they builded; ²⁹ but in the day that Lot went out from Sodom it rained fire and brimstone from heaven, and destroyed them all: ³⁰ after the same manner shall it be in the day that the Son of man is revealed. ³¹ In that day, he that shall be on the housetop, and his goods in the house, let him not go down to take them away: and let him that is in the field likewise not return back. ³² Remember Lot's wife. ³³ Whosoever shall seek to gain his life shall lose it: but whosoever shall lose his life shall preserve it. ³⁴ I say unto you, In that night there shall be two men on one bed; the one shall be taken, and the other shall be left. ³⁵ There shall be two women grinding together; the one shall be taken, and the other shall be left. ³⁷ And they answering say unto him, Where, Lord? And he said unto them, Where the body is, thither will the eagles also be gathered together.

Whosoever shall seek to gain his life shall lose it
Whosoever shall lose his life shall preserve it

The Savior one fine day announced

Leaving us to wonder
What he meant

Let go
And let God?

There's also
Let the good times roll
Not to mention
Let go
And fall off the cliff
Into nothingness

Whosoever seeks to gain his life
Shall lose it

Except in time
Everybody loses it

Like it or not
We all fall off the cliff

Basing a faith
Founded on truths
And half-truths
Truisms
And verities

A god-man
Becomes a sign of contradiction
Why wouldn't he?

This healer can't cure cancer
Or stop heart attacks

As children starve to death around the world
He rises from the dead

He'd have to
Otherwise

What's the point?

He hasn't been heard from in two thousand years
Except in dreams
And the steadfast accounts of
Determined evangelicals

We lose our lives
Then expend the rest of eternity
Finding them

If we ever do

The first rule of life is suffering
The second
Ignorance

Good thing

THE RENEWAL OF ALL THINGS

Matthew 19:16–30

[16] And behold, one came to him and said, Teacher, what good thing shall I do, that I may have eternal life? [17] And he said unto him, Why askest thou me concerning that which is good? One there is who is good: but if thou wouldest enter into life, keep the commandments. [18] He saith unto him, Which? And Jesus said, Thou shalt not kill, Thou shalt not commit adultery, Thou shalt not steal, Thou shalt not bear false witness, [19] Honor thy father and thy mother; and, Thou shalt love thy neighbor as thyself. [20] The young man saith unto him, All these things have I observed: what lack I yet? [21] Jesus said unto him, If thou wouldest be perfect, go, sell that which thou hast, and give to the poor, and thou shalt have treasure in heaven: and come, follow me. [22] But when the young man heard the saying, he went away sorrowful; for he was one that had great possessions.

[23] And Jesus said unto his disciples, Verily I say unto you, It is hard for a rich man to enter into the kingdom of heaven. [24] And again I say unto you, It is easier for a camel to go through a needle's eye, than for a rich man to enter into the kingdom of God. [25] And when the disciples heard it, they were astonished exceedingly, saying, Who then can be saved? [26] And Jesus looking upon them said to them, With men this is impossible; but with God all things are possible. [27] Then answered Peter and said unto him, Lo, we have left all, and followed thee; what then shall we have? [28] And Jesus said unto them, Verily I say unto you, that ye who have followed me, in the regeneration when the Son of man shall sit on the throne of his glory, ye also shall sit upon twelve thrones, judging the twelve tribes of Israel. [29] And every one that hath left houses, or brethren, or sisters, or father, or mother, or children, or lands, for my name's sake, shall receive a hundredfold, and shall inherit eternal life. [30] But many shall be last that are first; and first that are last.

Many shall be last that are first
And first that are last

He declared
Promising eternity
To those who would relinquish
Fields
Family
Friends
And the pursuit of wealth

One day a village carpenter
The next the King of Kings
Not to mention
His execution
And after that
Rising from the dead

One day a corpse
The next morning a celebrity

With God all things are possible

The story of Hollywood

Bit players moving up
From uncredited appearances
No dialogue
Meagre pay
Becoming megastars
Adored by multitudes
Until one fine day
These household gods
In the natural scheme of things

Fade to black
The End

He was a nobody
A nudnik mensch
At the far end of empire

With God all things are possible

All things
Meaning sacrifice
And the import of love

In which case
He lives forevermore

TWO BLIND MEN

Matthew 20:29–34

29 And as they went out from Jericho, a great multitude followed him. 30 And behold, two blind men sitting by the way side, when they heard that Jesus was passing by, cried out, saying, Lord, have mercy on us, thou son of David. 31 And the multitude rebuked them, that they should hold their peace: but they cried out the more, saying, Lord, have mercy on us, thou son of David. 32 And Jesus stood still, and called them, and said, What will ye that I should do unto you? 33 They say unto him, Lord, that our eyes may be opened. 34 And Jesus, being moved with compassion, touched their eyes; and straightway they received their sight, and followed him.

I was blind
And you touched me
For the first time
I could see

Blind
I saw nothing but
Souls
Heard heartbeats
Emotion rushing like the rain
I understood the welling up of grief
And gladness
Happy in my infirmity
Not understanding
How blessed I was

Why did you touch me?
Why would I ask you to open my eyes?
What was I thinking?

I never imagined ugliness

Bodies scarred
Missing limbs
Mottled teeth
Beauty run to fat

These days

I judge everyone
On how they look

I cannot help myself

I am ruined

And alone

ZACCHAEUS

Luke 19:1–10

¹ And he entered and was passing through Jericho. ² And behold, a man called by name Zacchæus; and he was a chief publican, and he was rich. ³ And he sought to see Jesus who he was; and could not for the crowd, because he was little of stature. ⁴ And he ran on before, and climbed up into a sycamore tree to see him: for he was to pass that way. ⁵ And when Jesus came to the place, he looked up, and said unto him, Zacchæus, make haste, and come down; for to-day I must abide at thy house. ⁶ And he made haste, and came down, and received him joyfully. ⁷ And when they saw it, they all murmured, saying, He is gone in to lodge with a man that is a sinner. ⁸ And Zacchæus stood, and said unto the Lord, Behold, Lord, the half of my goods I give to the poor; and if I have wrongfully exacted aught of any man, I restore fourfold. ⁹ And Jesus said unto him, To-day is salvation come to this house, forasmuch as he also is a son of Abraham. ¹⁰ For the Son of man came to seek and to save that which was lost.

Little of stature?
The man was short

Good thing he climbed into a sycamore
To witness this year's passing celebrity
A rabbi preaching peace and love
Countercultural before his time

Zacchaeus, come down

The rabbi said
Inviting himself to dine

"The man is a sinner"
Murmured the crowd
A publican
A tax collector
Hey!
What else you need to know?

Before they'd
Uncorked the wine
And broken bread
Zacchaeus pledged half his goods to the poor
Prompting Jesus to announce the man was saved

Adding
He had come to find those who were lost

Which has what to do
With you and me?

Are we lost too?

Should we hand over half our goods to the poor?

What about tomorrow
And the day after that?

The moral:
Never climb a sycamore
To spy on a passing celebrity

You may end up
Broke

And begging

Righteous doesn't pay the bills

JESUS COMES TO JERUSALEM AS KING

Matthew 21:1–9

¹ And when they drew nigh unto Jerusalem, and came unto Bethphage, unto the mount of Olives, then Jesus sent two disciples, ² saying unto them, Go into the village that is over against you, and straightway ye shall find an ass tied, and a colt with her: loose them, and bring them unto me. ³ And if any one say aught unto you, ye shall say, The Lord hath need of them; and straightway he will send them. ⁴ Now this is come to pass, that it might be fulfilled which was spoken through the prophet, saying,

> *⁵ Tell ye the daughter of Zion,*
> *Behold, thy King cometh unto thee,*
> *Meek, and riding upon an ass,*
> *And upon a colt the foal of an ass.*

⁶ And the disciples went, and did even as Jesus appointed them, ⁷ and brought the ass, and the colt, and put on them their garments; and he sat thereon. ⁸ And the most part of the multitude spread their garments in the way; and others cut branches from the trees, and spread them in the way. ⁹ And the multitudes that went before him, and that followed, cried, saying, Hosanna to the son of David: Blessed is he that cometh in the name of the Lord; Hosanna in the highest.

The king rides into town
Astride an ass
Ain't that a laugh!

Can't you see
The Supreme Allied Commander

President of the European Union
Joint Chiefs of Staff
President of these United
Trading in their limousines
For barnyard animals?

Attending crowds
Calling him blessed
Screaming Hosannas
Wow

What world is this?

In our mind's eye
Returning us to Bethlehem
To the stable
Surrounded by angels
Shepherds
And astrologers
Not to mention
Horses, donkeys, and dogs
All convinced
The Alpha and the Omega
The center of the surrounding universe
Born in a cattle shed
Was here

Hosanna
An outdated expression
Even then

Jesus rides to town sitting on an ass
The natural order of everything
Turned inside out
And upside down

For those who can see
Past stocks and bonds
And real estate

If this gesture is so significant
A revelation in its time
Apparently important even now

How come nobody's tried it since?

Political theatre?

Who's kidding whom?

THE COMMUNION

Matthew 26:26–29

26 And as they were eating, Jesus took bread, and blessed, and brake it; and he gave to the disciples, and said, Take, eat; this is my body. 27 And he took a cup, and gave thanks, and gave to them, saying, Drink ye all of it; 28 for this is my blood of the covenant, which is poured out for many unto the remission of sins. 29 But I say unto you, I shall not drink henceforth of this fruit of the vine, until that day when I drink it new with you in my Father's kingdom.

This is my body
Take ye and eat

Rings down through the centuries
Outperforming Aztec sacrifice
Roman gladiators
Coriolanus
And World War Two

This is my body
Take ye and eat

He said again
Prompting
Billions who believe
To line up
And consume the flesh
Of God

For this is my blood of the covenant
Which is poured out for many unto the remission of sins

Once more
Multitudes
Stand in line
To drink the blood of the sanctified

Communion
Outperforming
Beatles
Golden Globes
Alibaba
Amazon
Even the Aryan Race

So great becomes our longing
To be one with one another
One with the earth
One with all the gods
Who ever ruled the universe
And the hearts of humankind

This is our body
This is our blood

Communion is our name

Amen

THE SPIRIT IS WILLING

Matthew 26:31–52

31 Then saith Jesus unto them, All ye shall be offended in me this night: for it is written, I will smite the shepherd, and the sheep of the flock shall be scattered abroad. 32 But after I am raised up, I will go before you into Galilee. 33 But Peter answered and said unto him, If all shall be offended in thee, I will never be offended. 34 Jesus said unto him, Verily I say unto thee, that this night, before the cock crow, thou shalt deny me thrice. 35 Peter saith unto him, Even if I must die with thee, yet will I not deny thee. Likewise also said all the disciples.

36 Then cometh Jesus with them unto a place called Gethsemane, and saith unto his disciples, Sit ye here, while I go yonder and pray. 37 And he took with him Peter and the two sons of Zebedee, and began to be sorrowful and sore troubled. 38 Then saith he unto them, My soul is exceeding sorrowful, even unto death: abide ye here, and watch with me. 39 And he went forward a little, and fell on his face, and prayed, saying, My Father, if it be possible, let this cup pass away from me: nevertheless, not as I will, but as thou wilt. 40 And he cometh unto the disciples, and findeth them sleeping, and saith unto Peter, What, could ye not watch with me one hour? 41 Watch and pray, that ye enter not into temptation: the spirit indeed is willing, but the flesh is weak.

42 Again a second time he went away, and prayed, saying, My Father, if this cannot pass away, except I drink it, thy will be done. 43 And he came again and found them sleeping, for their eyes were heavy. 44 And he left them again, and went away, and prayed a third time, saying again the same words. 45 Then cometh he to the disciples, and saith unto them, Sleep on now, and take your rest: behold, the hour is at hand, and the Son *of man is betrayed into the hands of sinners. * [46] *Arise, let us be going: behold, he is at hand that betrayeth me.*

[47] *And while he yet spake, lo, Judas, one of the twelve, came, and with him a great multitude with swords and staves, from the chief priests and elders of the people. * [48] *Now he that betrayed him gave them a sign, saying, Whomsoever I shall kiss, that is he: take him. * [49] *And straightway he came to Jesus, and said, Hail, Rabbi; and kissed him. * [50] *And Jesus said unto him, Friend, do that for which thou art come. Then they came and laid hands on Jesus, and took him. * [51] *And behold, one of them that were with Jesus stretched out his hand, and drew his sword, and smote the servant of the high priest, and struck off his ear. * [52] *Then saith Jesus unto him, Put up again thy sword into its place: for all they that take the sword shall perish with the sword.*

The Spirit indeed
Is willing
But the flesh is weak

Indeed

The story of the human race

We rise in our dreams
To glory
Invoking light
Summoning angels
To lead us into symphonies of grace
At least
To equilibrium

Who is this Jesus
Who orders us
To watch with him
On the edge

Of sacrifice?

To watch for what?

Generations have proclaimed
He died for our sins

His blood
Our redeeming grace

What sins we say?

We are born in deprivation
The prophets remembering
The ever-present fall of Man
How else to explain
Our cruelty?
Our ignorance?

Why so many questions
Even now

Maybe the spirit is unwilling too

JUDAS

Matthew 27:1–10

¹ *Now when morning was come, all the chief priests and the elders of the people took counsel against Jesus to put him to death:* ² *and they bound him, and led him away, and delivered him up to Pilate the governor.*

³ *Then Judas, who betrayed him, when he saw that he was condemned, repented himself, and brought back the thirty pieces of silver to the chief priests and elders,* ⁴ *saying, I have sinned in that I betrayed innocent blood. But they said, What is that to us? see thou to it.* ⁵ *And he cast down the pieces of silver into the sanctuary, and departed; and he went away and hanged himself.* ⁶ *And the chief priests took the pieces of silver, and said, It is not lawful to put them into the treasury, since it is the price of blood.* ⁷ *And they took counsel, and bought with them the potter's field, to bury strangers in.* ⁸ *Wherefore that field was called, The field of blood, unto this day.* ⁹ *Then was fulfilled that which was spoken through Jeremiah the prophet, saying, And they took the thirty pieces of silver, the price of him that was priced, whom certain of the children of Israel did price;* ¹⁰ *and they gave them for the potter's field, as the Lord appointed me.*

Remember your Judas
Everybody has one

Out of nowhere
You are betrayed
Your sins
Revealed

Your secrets transmitted
To the waiting world

Is it a he
Or a she
Thrilled to take you down?

Does he feel so bad about himself
He exults in toppling you?

Who has time to psychoanalyze
Pain
To investigate duplicity
Or even give it a name?

All you can say is
I thought you were a friend
And love him
Or is it a her?

And let them go

Into their own night

GETHSEMANE

Matthew 26:36–41

36 Then cometh Jesus with them unto a place called Gethsemane, and saith unto his disciples, Sit ye here, while I go yonder and pray. 37 And he took with him Peter and the two sons of Zebedee, and began to be sorrowful and sore troubled. 38 Then saith he unto them, My soul is exceeding sorrowful, even unto death: abide ye here, and watch with me. 39 And he went forward a little, and fell on his face, and prayed, saying, My Father, if it be possible, let this cup pass away from me: nevertheless, not as I will, but as thou wilt. 40 And he cometh unto the disciples, and findeth them sleeping, and saith unto Peter, What, could ye not watch with me one hour? 41 Watch and pray, that ye enter not into temptation: the spirit indeed is willing, but the flesh is weak.

He walks with me, and He talks with me,
And He tells me I am His own

In the Garden
Goes my mother's favorite hymn

He did talk to her apparently
Or so she said

The question is
Who talked to him?

He said
She would carry her cross

She wondered when

The dread of not knowing
How much pain awaits
How much death
How much despair
And disrepair

Even the most enlightened
Cannot flee the dark

Christ is crucified until the end of time
According to St. Paul
A scandal to the fundamentalists
Demanding
He rise into light
Almost immediately

Otherwise
What's the point?

For the rest of us
Resurgence lurks in shadow
We remain unaware
Of who we are
And who we are meant to be
Buoyed
Only by inference
And myth

And sometimes
Yes
By one among us
Who says he's already come and gone
And will surely come again

To walk with us
And talk with us
And tell us

We are his own

THY WILL BE DONE

Matthew 26:40–46

⁴⁰ And he cometh unto the disciples, and findeth them sleeping, and saith unto Peter, What, could ye not watch with me one hour? ⁴¹ Watch and pray, that ye enter not into temptation: the spirit indeed is willing, but the flesh is weak. ⁴² Again a second time he went away, and prayed, saying, My Father, if this cannot pass away, except I drink it, thy will be done. ⁴³ And he came again and found them sleeping, for their eyes were heavy. ⁴⁴ And he left them again, and went away, and prayed a third time, saying again the same words. ⁴⁵ Then cometh he to the disciples, and saith unto them, Sleep on now, and take your rest: behold, the hour is at hand, and the Son of man is betrayed into the hands of sinners. ⁴⁶ Arise, let us be going: behold, he is at hand that betrayeth me.

The spirit indeed is willing
But the flesh is weak

Our spirits
Cannot overcome the flesh
We were made this way

Feeding our faces
Drinking into oblivion
Abandoning gods and goddesses
For an extra fifty bucks

Face it
We were fashioned

For swimming pools
And sex
The kick of the moment
The thrill of the chase
Worshipping beauty
Evading death

We are put upon
Shamed
Reviled for being corporeal
We eat
Sleep
And copulate too much

Supposedly defying God
Who made us
Exactly as we are

Or so we are told

On the other hand

Decide

Did we create ourselves?

JESUS IS CONDEMNED

Luke 22:66–71

⁶⁶ And as soon as it was day, the assembly of the elders of the people was gathered together, both chief priests and scribes; and they led him away into their council, saying, ⁶⁷ If thou art the Christ, tell us. But he said unto them, If I tell you, ye will not believe: ⁶⁸ and if I ask you, ye will not answer. ⁶⁹ But from henceforth shall the Son of man be seated at the right hand of the power of God. ⁷⁰ And they all said, Art thou then the Son of God? And he said unto them, Ye say that I am. ⁷¹ And they said, What further need have we of witness? for we ourselves have heard from his own mouth.

Who is the Son of God?
Is it Jesus Christ?

Or is it everyone alive
Or for that matter dead?

What is our inheritance?

Dare we affirm
The kingdom is within
As we've been told
Or is that a message on a greeting card?

To assert we are the sons of God
Would imply

Each of us is consecrated
And inviolable

How does that translate
To the courts
The prisons
And social media?

Or is being a child of God
More a question
For ourselves?

Where does veneration
For the soul begin
If not with us?

You are the temples of the Holy Ghost
Said Sister Mary Immaculate

That would be us
Uncomprehending
And rightfully
Unaware

Translated
God bless the child
That's got his own

You and me

Undoubtedly

Perhaps in the end
We will understand
These terms

These claims
These hypotheticals
That wander well past sense
Blurring all significance

Leaving us overwhelmed
With somebody else's meaning

Wondering about our own

PETER'S DENIAL

Matthew 26:69–75

⁶⁹ *Now Peter was sitting without in the court: and a maid came unto him, saying, Thou also wast with Jesus the Galilæan.* ⁷⁰ *But he denied before them all, saying, I know not what thou sayest.* ⁷¹ *And when he was gone out into the porch, another maid saw him, and saith unto them that were there, This man also was with Jesus of Nazareth.* ⁷² *And again he denied with an oath, I know not the man.* ⁷³ *And after a little while they that stood by came and said to Peter, Of a truth thou also art one of them; for thy speech maketh thee known.* ⁷⁴ *Then began he to curse and to swear, I know not the man. And straightway the cock crew.* ⁷⁵ *And Peter remembered the word which Jesus had said, Before the cock crow, thou shalt deny me thrice. And he went out, and wept bitterly.*

Our Judases
Betray us
Out of jealousy
We more or less expected that
They remain a common breed

But Peter
A friend beyond friends
Broke us at our core
Denying he knew us
"Friends forever"
He had repeated
A thousand times

Out of fear
For his life
Apparently
Delivering us to
Executioners
And thugs

How else to describe them?

The killers of
Everything we hold dear

Why does the ordinary man
Women too
Feed on anxiety
The cancer
That grows in our souls
Defiling the promises of life

And why do I?

Common as a garden snake
Slithering through weeds
Never far from being terrified
All the while
Pretending otherwise

Peter is us

Me and you

Every day

In every way

Ain't that so?

PILATE

Mark 15:1–15

¹ And straightway in the morning the chief priests with the elders and scribes, and the whole council, held a consultation, and bound Jesus, and carried him away, and delivered him up to Pilate. ² And Pilate asked him, Art thou the King of the Jews? And he answering saith unto him, Thou sayest. ³ And the chief priests accused him of many things. ⁴ And Pilate again asked him, saying, Answerest thou nothing? behold how many things they accuse thee of. ⁵ But Jesus no more answered anything; insomuch that Pilate marvelled.

⁶ Now at the feast he used to release unto them one prisoner, whom they asked of him. ⁷ And there was one called Barabbas, lying bound with them that had made insurrection, men who in the insurrection had committed murder. ⁸ And the multitude went up and began to ask him to do as he was wont to do unto them. ⁹ And Pilate answered them, saying, Will ye that I release unto you the King of the Jews? ¹⁰ For he perceived that for envy the chief priests had delivered him up. ¹¹ But the chief priests stirred up the multitude, that he should rather release Barabbas unto them. ¹² And Pilate again answered and said unto them, What then shall I do unto him whom ye call the King of the Jews? ¹³ And they cried out again, Crucify him. ¹⁴ And Pilate said unto them, Why, what evil hath he done? But they cried out exceedingly, Crucify him. ¹⁵ And Pilate, wishing to content the multitude, released unto them Barabbas, and delivered Jesus, when he had scourged him, to be crucified.

Pilate

Whatever you do

Protect your political career

In short order
Execute anyone
Who intimidates the government

Don't imagine for a minute
You are caving to the crowd

In all respects
You sustain the common will
Which is to say
The state
Without which we would disintegrate
And be destroyed

Jesus
The King of the Jews
The one group
With a God
That judges history

When did they ever colonize
Or subjugate?

Jews are devoted
To reason
Law
Morality
Justice for the poor
Not to mention
Seventh Avenue
Hollywood
Bright lights
And ballyhoo
All of it

Adults in the room
Enjoy!

Ask this king in front of you
How best to live
Ask him how to occupy the earth

He knows

Ask him to bless you

If you dare

THE CROWN OF THORNS

John 19:1–3

¹ Then Pilate therefore took Jesus, and scourged him. ² And the soldiers platted a crown of thorns, and put it on his head, and arrayed him in a purple garment; ³ and they came unto him, and said, Hail, King of the Jews! and they struck him with their hands.

The crown of thorns
Would indicate the brain
The head
The face
Is this a metaphor?

At the center
Of everything we are
We struggle to recognize
Where we have come from
And where we are going

The subtext
One of pain
And confusion

The solution
Have another drink
Go to the movies
Rent a DVD

Listen to hip hop
Enjoy it while you can

The man is dripping blood
Utterly uncivilized

Go with bright light
And a simple cross
Forget the crucifix
What do we believe in anyway
If not clean lines
And good design?

Scourged
There's a word

What about waterboarding
Or the rack
Hang the prisoner upside down
Draw and quarter him
Ditch him in an unmarked grave

Did you bring the lavender
To disinfect the dead?

Through Jesus Christ

Amen

JESUS BEARS THE CROSS

John 19:6–16

⁶ *When therefore the chief priests and the officers saw him, they cried out, saying, Crucify him, crucify him! Pilate saith unto them, Take him yourselves, and crucify him: for I find no crime in him.* ⁷ *The Jews answered him, We have a law, and by that law he ought to die, because he made himself the Son of God.* ⁸ *When Pilate therefore heard this saying, he was the more afraid;* ⁹ *and he entered into the Prætorium again, and saith unto Jesus, Whence art thou? But Jesus gave him no answer.* ¹⁰ *Pilate therefore saith unto him, Speakest thou not unto me? knowest thou not that I have power to release thee, and have power to crucify thee?* ¹¹ *Jesus answered him, Thou wouldest have no power against me, except it were given thee from above: therefore he that delivered me unto thee hath greater sin.* ¹² *Upon this Pilate sought to release him: but the Jews cried out, saying, If thou release this man, thou art not Cæsar's friend: every one that maketh himself a king speaketh against Cæsar.* ¹³ *When Pilate therefore heard these words, he brought Jesus out, and sat down on the judgment-seat at a place called The Pavement, but in Hebrew, Gabbatha.* ¹⁴ *Now it was the Preparation of the passover: it was about the sixth hour. And he saith unto the Jews, Behold, your King!* ¹⁵ *They therefore cried out, Away with him, away with him, crucify him! Pilate saith unto them, Shall I crucify your King? The chief priests answered, We have no king but Cæsar.* ¹⁶ *Then therefore he delivered him unto them to be crucified.*

You will always have a cross to bear
My Nana said
When we got too big for our britches

She said
You'll see

We wanted everything
She said
All of it
Beauty
Money
Love

Impossible

With the War
Whichever one
The Depression
Too many deaths to bear
She buried children
Dealt with betrayal
Slander
False friends
And smiling enemies

That would never happen to us
We said
We knew how to win friends and influence people
We were the American Dream
We thought positive thoughts
Didn't we?
Focusing on what we wanted
Yay

Our mantra
Nothing could stop us
Except of course
More war

More betrayal
More deceit

That wouldn't be us

And loss of faith
Oh that

Fires die
Rivers overflow their banks
Spirits explode like falling stars

Where does life come from anyway?
Why so much contradiction
Why loss?

Why silence
In the face of
Questioning?

Why the cross?

Nana
Are you there?

SIMON THE CYRENIAN

Mark 15:21

[21] *And they compel one passing by, Simon of Cyrene, coming from the country, the father of Alexander and Rufus, to go with them, that he might bear his cross.*

Who will help me carry my cross?
Who will see me through my pain?

We are intertwined
Interconnected
Overlapping
Souls
They say

Why do I block you?
Why do I pretend
I am singular?

Why do I shut out the light
Trusting the night
For its absolute simplicity?

There is nothing in the dark
But emptiness
And a trillion galaxies
Too far away to touch

Help me open my arms
To you

If I will not release my heart

Abandon me

Until I do

THE WOMEN OF JERUSALEM

Luke 23:27–31

27 And there followed him a great multitude of the people, and of women who bewailed and lamented him. 28 But Jesus turning unto them said, Daughters of Jerusalem, weep not for me, but weep for yourselves, and for your children. 29 For behold, the days are coming, in which they shall say, Blessed are the barren, and the wombs that never bare, and the breasts that never gave suck. 30 Then shall they begin to say to the mountains, Fall on us; and to the hills, Cover us. 31 For if they do these things in the green tree, what shall be done in the dry?

Weep not for me
I be fine

Weep for the world
And the sorrows
You will never understand
Except to embrace
All of it
Yes
The whole shebang

Look upon the faces of your little ones
Enfold the battlefield
Applaud the majesty of art
And razzmatazz
That's it

Rejoice in laughter
Where you find it
And weep for the end of who we are

Weep not for me

Weep for yourselves

And your children

Weep for generations yet unborn
And born again
Pogroms and kristallnachts
Bergen-Belsens
Sistine Chapels
Golden Globes
And Mardi Gras

Weep for the great unwashed
Who revile the seers of Israel
Crying out for justice
And a level playing field

That means a living wage
Hear hear!

Weep for your descendants
And the world they will embrace

Weep not for me
I ascend into light
Having delivered my body
To the dogs of night

Weep for yourselves
Born into servitude

Trapped in unknowing

Weep for the love
You will never know

Until one day
One day soon enough
You too
Will ascend in light

I will be expecting you

THE CRUCIFIX

The crucifix
Definitive bad taste
Akin to photographs of
Abu Ghraib
Hiroshima
Auschwitz
And El Salvador

Would you want one
Hanging in your living room
Except perhaps as installation art
Intended to provoke

Where is the revelation of divinity
In pain?

Suffering withholds its soul
Until the heart implodes
And reason atrophies

Out of ashes
And the night
Comes whatever meaning we decide

Perhaps we need to concentrate on
More distracting things
Jacarandas blossoming
Newborn kangaroos
That's fun

Colonies of seals
Auroral borealis
All things bright
And whispering

The ferocity of life
Unstoppable

Transporting us away from Calvary
Into the miracle of birth

Why do we obsess so much
On an executed criminal
Insisting he's divinity
Despite himself?

More to the point
Why are we preoccupied with death?

In the meantime

The jury is out

JESUS IS CRUCIFIED

Luke 23:33–38

³³ And when they came unto the place which is called The skull, there they crucified him, and the malefactors, one on the right hand and the other on the left. ³⁴ And Jesus said, Father, forgive them; for they know not what they do. And parting his garments among them, they cast lots. ³⁵ And the people stood beholding. And the rulers also scoffed at him, saying, He saved others; let him save himself, if this is the Christ of God, his chosen. ³⁶ And the soldiers also mocked him, coming to him, offering him vinegar, ³⁷ and saying, If thou art the King of the Jews, save thyself. ³⁸ And there was also a superscription over him, THIS IS THE KING OF THE JEWS.

The crucifix
Hangs above my bed
Said the king of a country
Long since disappeared
Under smoke and violence
And improbable improvement
Nothing like the wars to end all wars

In this sign you will conquer
Said Constantine the Great
Emperor
Conqueror
Murderer
Referring to the cross
Turned inside out

And upside down

If it's not Christian
Burn it to the ground

Gentle Jesus
What have they done to you?

Your death has
Opened doors to
Perversity
Did you know not know this
Going in?

Father forgive them
For they know not what they do

You said it first

Last

And always

THE GOOD THIEF

Luke 23:39–43

³⁹ *And one of the malefactors that were hanged railed on him, saying, Art not thou the Christ? save thyself and us.* ⁴⁰ *But the other answered, and rebuking him said, Dost thou not even fear God, seeing thou art in the same condemnation?* ⁴¹ *And we indeed justly; for we receive the due reward of our deeds: but this man hath done nothing amiss.* ⁴² *And he said, Jesus, remember me when thou comest in thy kingdom.* ⁴³ *And he said unto him, Verily I say unto thee, To-day shalt thou be with me in Paradise.*

Today
Shalt thou be with me in Paradise

Said Jesus to the Good Thief

He died on the cross right next to him
Love alive in his crooked heart
Ain't that the truth
The only truth
Yes Ma'am

Love reaching out to love
Don't that sound original
Face it
Sometimes simplicity cuts through shit
Revelation arrives
When you're least expecting it

Remember me
Said the Good Thief

How could we forget?

JESUS SPEAKS TO HIS MOTHER AND THE DISCIPLE

John 19:25–27

²⁵ These things therefore the soldiers did. But there were standing by the cross of Jesus his mother, and his mother's sister, Mary the wife of Clopas, and Mary Magdalene. ²⁶ When Jesus therefore saw his mother, and the disciple standing by whom he loved, he saith unto his mother, Woman, behold, thy son! ²⁷ Then saith he to the disciple, Behold, thy mother! And from that hour the disciple took her unto his own home.

Blessed Mother
Madonna
Mary Immaculate
Star of the Sea
Queen of Heaven
Mother of Mercy
Mater Amabilis
A hundred names
In too many languages to count

All of the above
Adding imagination
And fantasy
To an artless village woman
Standing by her son
A rabbi executed by the state
Between two thieves

He was
Apparently
A threat to order
And stability
In that colonial outpost
Of imperial Rome

Consider the Congo under King Leopold
Johannesburg under the Boers
The Trail of Tears
Haiti
Birkenau
Skibbereen

The list is long

The beat goes on

We die for each other's sins

With our mothers standing by

THE SIXTH HOUR

Luke 23:44–46

⁴⁴ And it was now about the sixth hour, and a darkness came over the whole land until the ninth hour, ⁴⁵ the sun's light failing: and the veil of the temple was rent in the midst. ⁴⁶ And Jesus, crying with a loud voice, said, Father, into thy hands I commend my spirit: and having said this, he gave up the ghost.

Father forgive them
For they know not what they do

That was worth mentioning
Can we say the same
About our very own
Architects of death
Consider the Armenian massacres
The Third Reich
Gulags
Pol Pot
Mao
Who is inviolable?

When does it end?

For they know not what they do

We are surrounded by scientists
Who disregard
Any overriding intelligence

Or the invisible substance
Of universal love

Hospital patients
Regularly succumb to MRSA
Flesh eating bacteria
And overprescribed opioids

Children carry Uzis
Ak-47s
And Kalashnikovs
Into elementary schools

For they know not what they do

Two hundred fifty years of slavery
Rampant pedophilia
A litany of hopelessness

Sorry to ruin dinner
Sorry to step on local wit

Where's Groucho
Chico
Harpo
These days
On Calvary?

Rest assured
They're here
Everybody's here

Laughter
The brightest light

Of God
Real or imagined

Bozo
Clarabelle
Pierrot
Scaramouche
Oberon
Titania
Harlequin
And fairy queens

And the rest of us clowns
Hair plugged
Nose jobbed
Gastric bypassed
Bronzed to die
And dyed to match

We're still figuring it out

Amen

JESUS DIES ON THE CROSS

Luke 23:44–46 (Once again)

⁴⁴ And it was now about the sixth hour, and a darkness came over the whole land until the ninth hour, ⁴⁵ the sun's light failing: and the veil of the temple was rent in the midst. ⁴⁶ And Jesus, crying with a loud voice, said, Father, into thy hands I commend my spirit: and having said this, he gave up the ghost.

Jesus dies on the cross
The center
Of the known
And unknown universe

Crucifixes
Hanging above a billion beds
Along with JFK
And Dr. King
He gazes out
With unrelenting love
Ain't that the point?

Why get into particulars
Of blood and pain
And betrayal?
His center holds
If ours has since ignited
On a thousand battlefields

Along with shattered sympathies
Of violated nuns
And broken pietas

At his feet
Buddha
Mary Magdalen
Osiris too
Zeus
Diana
Dionysus
Father Abraham
Our pantheon

Their minds resolute on us
Fanatics
Atheists
Schizophrenic
Us

The first rule of life is suffering
The second rule
Sacrifice

In the meantime

What about love?

THE KING OF THE JEWS

Matthew 27:27–44

²⁷ *Then the soldiers of the governor took Jesus into the Prœ-torium, and gathered unto him the whole band.* ²⁸ *And they stripped him, and put on him a scarlet robe.* ²⁹ *And they platted a crown of thorns and put it upon his head, and a reed in his right hand; and they kneeled down before him, and mocked him, saying, Hail, King of the Jews!* ³⁰ *And they spat upon him, and took the reed and smote him on the head.* ³¹ *And when they had mocked him, they took off from him the robe, and put on him his garments, and led him away to crucify him.*

³² *And as they came out, they found a man of Cyrene, Simon by name: him they compelled to go with them, that he might bear his cross.*

³³ *And when they were come unto a place called Golgotha, that is to say, The place of a skull,* ³⁴ *they gave him wine to drink mingled with gall: and when he had tasted it, he would not drink.* ³⁵ *And when they had crucified him, they parted his garments among them, casting lots;* ³⁶ *and they sat and watched him there.* ³⁷ *And they set up over his head his accusation written, THIS IS JESUS THE KING OF THE JEWS.* ³⁸ *Then are there crucified with him two robbers, one on the right hand and one on the left.* ³⁹ *And they that passed by railed on him, wagging their heads,* ⁴⁰ *and saying, Thou that destroyest the temple, and buildest it in three days, save thyself: if thou art the Son of God, come down from the cross.* ⁴¹ *In like manner also the chief priests mocking him, with the scribes and elders, said,* ⁴² *He saved others; himself he cannot save. He is the King of Israel; let him now come down from the cross, and we will believe on him.* ⁴³ *He trust-eth on God; let him deliver him now, if he desireth him: for he*

said, I am the Son of God. [44] *And the robbers also that were crucified with him cast upon him the same reproach.*

He trusted in God
Let God deliver him
They said
They the common denominator
The conventional wisdom
We

If there's a God
He will rescue you
From empires
Be they Roman
Or the Reich
Not to mention social media

Universal consciousness
Love and compassion
If you believe in that
Has no intention of intervention

We bloom as the flowers in spring
Coming in from the cold

Spellbinding
For a time

Before we wither
And blow away
Chasing after winds and rain
Into the eternal night

Do we invent mythologies
And gods
To deal with death
And the end of everything?

Do we?

Do you know?

MY GOD MY GOD

Matthew 27:45–46

⁴⁵ Now from the sixth hour there was darkness over all the land until the ninth hour. ⁴⁶ And about the ninth hour Jesus cried with a loud voice, saying, Eli, Eli, lama sabachthani? that is, My God, my God, why hast thou forsaken me?

My God
My God
Why hast thou forsaken me?

Said the Kulaks in Ukraine
And certainly Siberia

Said the six million massacred for what?

We keep returning to the obvious
The cruelty of man
The unrescued
The mutilated children
All for someone's notion
Of a great society
Good luck

If there be no original sin
There sure be blockage
In the reckoning
And in the perception
Of who we are

Evolution
So-called
Becomes incomprehensible
Except to scientists

And even they
Turn out to be
Trapped in
Nothingness

Dachau
Auschwitz
Bergen-Belsen
Theresienstadt
You know the rest
Et cetera
Sinners
Intermittent geniuses
Six million
Friends and neighbors
Lovers
Dead

One to another
We are wired
With different attributes

There will always be kings
Type A comes in the DNA

Are we made to be fighting
With ourselves
And God
As we imagine him?

Are we fashioned
To be forsaken in the end?

Are we put on trial
For our beginnings
And our ends

For what?

My God
My God

That says it all

THE TOMB

Matthew 27:57–61

57 And when even was come, there came a rich man from Arimathæa, named Joseph, who also himself was Jesus' disciple: 58 this man went to Pilate, and asked for the body of Jesus. Then Pilate commanded it to be given up. 59 And Joseph took the body, and wrapped it in a clean linen cloth, 60 and laid it in his own new tomb, which he had hewn out in the rock: and he rolled a great stone to the door of the tomb, and departed. 61 And Mary Magdalene was there, and the other Mary, sitting over against the sepulchre.

Grant us compassion
When we are most in need
When we are dead to ourselves
And to the world

Grant us mercy
For our multiple sins
And omissions
The poor we have always among us
We know that well

We have neglected
The kingdom of heaven
Within
We have squandered our natural inheritance

Grant us forgiveness
For taking for granted
The beauty of Gaia
And the friendship
Of everything alive

Grant us love
To quicken us
As we lay in the grave
That we may once again
Rise into light

And once again
Learn to be alive

In the name of all that is

Forevermore

RESURRECTION

Matthew 28:1–10

¹ *Now late on the sabbath day, as it began to dawn toward the first day of the week, came Mary Magdalene and the other Mary to see the sepulchre.* ² *And behold, there was a great earthquake; for an angel of the Lord descended from heaven, and came and rolled away the stone, and sat upon it.* ³ *His appearance was as lightning, and his raiment white as snow:* ⁴ *and for fear of him the watchers did quake, and became as dead men.* ⁵ *And the angel answered and said unto the women, Fear not ye; for I know that ye seek Jesus, who hath been crucified.* ⁶ *He is not here; for he is risen, even as he said. Come, see the place where the Lord lay.* ⁷ *And go quickly, and tell his disciples, He is risen from the dead; and lo, he goeth before you into Galilee; there shall ye see him: lo, I have told you.* ⁸ *And they departed quickly from the tomb with fear and great joy, and ran to bring his disciples word.* ⁹ *And behold, Jesus met them, saying, All hail. And they came and took hold of his feet, and worshipped him.* ¹⁰ *Then saith Jesus unto them, Fear not: go tell my brethren that they depart into Galilee, and there shall they see me.*

Christ is risen
Alleluia

What does that have to do
With you and me?

Is Easter but a story
For those who fear the dark
Before the end of days?

Renaissance
Rebirth
The theme of winter
Evolving into spring
We die and come again
And yet again
Until we understand
The immortal I
Will never die

I stand before the light
Within my soul
Wondering from whence it comes
And where it goes

When I wander through the never-ending night
I hope to God
The light
Goes with me
Incandescent
And alive

And to my beloved atheists
Despising my plan
Ridiculing my intent
I say nothing at all

I know in my soul
What I know

My understanding
Remains innate

I never pretended to be rational

Or wise

Or otherwise

Amen

I AM WITH YOU

Matthew 28:18–20

18 And Jesus came to them and spake unto them, saying, All authority hath been given unto me in heaven and on earth. 19 Go ye therefore, and make disciples of all the nations, baptizing them into the name of the Father and of the Son and of the Holy Spirit: 20 teaching them to observe all things whatsoever I commanded you: and lo, I am with you always, even unto the end of the world.

He is with us
All days
Even to the consummation of the world

The story
Too close to Mithras
Isis
And Osiris
Especially this business
Of rising from the dead

Can we suspect
This narrative
Has been tinkered with
Adapted
Compromised?

To whose advantage
Are these absolutes?

Observing all things

Containing all authority

In heaven and on earth

Who grabs hold of these imperatives?

The Inquisition once again?
What about the Puritans?
Burning witches
Heretics
Astrologers
To cleanse the world
Of heathens
Real or imagined
Who refuse to bow down
Before the Vatican
And Plymouth Rock

Are Buddha
Mohammed
And the Egyptian deities with us too
Even to the consummation of the world
Why not?

At the moment
The conceit's
A parade of promises
A cornucopia of needs

As we sit here in the dark

Waiting

Wondering

Where are the gods today?

And Jesus
By the way

Are you with us now?

You with your infinite love for everyone
You the healer
The nurturer
The binder of wounds
And broken hearts

What have we done to you?

DOUBTING THOMAS

John 20:24–29

24 But Thomas, one of the twelve, called Didymus, was not with them when Jesus came. 25 The other disciples therefore said unto him, We have seen the Lord. But he said unto them, Except I shall see in his hands the print of the nails, and put my finger into the print of the nails, and put my hand into his side, I will not believe.

26 And after eight days again his disciples were within, and Thomas with them. Jesus cometh, the doors being shut, and stood in the midst, and said, Peace be unto you. 27 Then saith he to Thomas, Reach hither thy finger, and see my hands; and reach hither thy hand, and put it into my side: and be not faithless, but believing. 28 Thomas answered and said unto him, My Lord and my God. 29 Jesus saith unto him, Because thou hast seen me, thou hast believed: blessed are they that have not seen, and yet have believed.

Except I shall see in his hands the print of the nails
And put my finger into the print of the nails
And put my hand into his side
I will not believe

Said doubting Thomas
No fool he

The rest of us
Take somebody else's word for it
Meaning him
The renegade carpenter

Executed by the state
For possible insurrection
Or just by talking too much
The felony never quite clear

How could we forget
His rising from the dead

He did
At least somebody said he did
In a flash
Creating Chartres
Notre Dame
Michelangelo
Francis of Assisi
Assorted saints and cathedrals
Mozart's Mass in C Minor
And no doubt
Blessed Sacrament in Chevy Chase

Is that so?
Said the village atheist
The defector nun
And assorted altar boys
Betrayed by priestly pedophiles

Bless their hearts
All those who believe in gods
Capable of overriding flesh
And returning from the dead
Shazam!

This in the realm of the burning bush
The Immaculate Conception
Angelic announcements in Bethlehem

And yes Resurrection

A man of sorrow and simple joy
Could never be enough
Apparently

Doubting Thomas
Understood too well
Our cries in the night

And the expletives of earth

RESURRECTION ONCE AGAIN

Is resurrection
But a metaphor?
A leap of faith
Signifying
Life renews itself
Until the sun burns out?

Are we meant to see
Sinew
Muscle
Teeth
Once dead
And near to sludge
Suddenly catch their breath again?

Is that the question?

Death arrives
Like a thief in the night
He said

The band stops
Nearer my god to Thee

The brain goes numb
Power dies at Auschwitz
Hiroshima goes dark

In the next breath

Carnival erupts
Colored lights
Blaze forth
New generations
Holler again

Hallelujah baby

And then we die again

We do

And once again await the spring

MIRACLES

He is the miracle
His heart set on justice
Peace
Compassion
Care

Abstractions translated
Into food for the hungry
And shelter for the desperate

Why must those who chronicle his heart
Wander afield
Into walking on water
And multiplying loaves of bread
To feed the multitudes?

When it came to crucifixion
Angels did not rescue him

His agony remained
His torment real

Flesh remains resolute
Unyielding
In its primal density

The sacred heart
Was not enough
To offer proof of God

We have danced through miracles
And ancient songs
Recounted prophets
Raising up the dead

Why do we need miracles?
Can we not heal the sick ourselves?
Offer mercy to the desperate
Feed the hungry
Clothe the naked
And find the disappeared?

MARY

Who is this Mary
Catholics call the Mother of God?

In sanctuaries across the world
Gussied up in plaster blue
She stands triumphant on the globe
Stars encircling her painted head
A serpent coiled beneath her feet

Long way up from Nazareth

These days
Center stage
Guadalupe
Fatima
Medjugorje
Lourdes

Who are you
Mary Immaculate?

Are you the marble mother in the Pieta?
The lady in The Song of Bernadette?

Every day
We pray
Holy Mary Mother of God
By the way
Which God is that?

A village girl
Fourteen at the Nativity
They say
Impregnated by the Holy Ghost
A question asked in all sincerity:
Was God a pedophile?

Once again
We subvert the messenger
And betray the truth

Our God today is sheathed in gold
The Mother of God a queen

Once again
We return to intimations of royalty
To explain our deities

None of which works

Never did

Never will

EPILOGUE

Twenty centuries afterwards
We ask again
What happened here
Once upon a time
In Israel?

Is Jesus Christ
The way
The life
The truth?
Do we need only call his name?

And then what?

To be notified
According to St. Paul
We too will bear our cross
Until the end of time?

Where is joy across the land?
Where is Jesus when the sparrow falls?
When does love walk right in
And chase the shadows away
That is to say
When conquering armies
Commit unspeakable crimes?

Where is the good news of salvation?

Incidentally
By the way
Tell us once again
We are saved from what?
From the life
He too led
On the edge of empire
Governed by militias
And sometime psychopaths
Bounded by the suffering
Of the haunted human race?

We carry on
We do
Bearing shards of hope
Recollections of laughter
Memories of falling in love

All this
Between breakfast and lunch
And anti-depressants

As for the rest of it
God
Eternal life
Beatific vision
Yada yada

Stop

The moment is now

A NEW HEAVEN AND A NEW EARTH

Revelation 21:1–8

¹ *And I saw a new heaven and a new earth: for the first heaven and the first earth are passed away; and the sea is no more.* ² *And I saw the holy city, new Jerusalem, coming down out of heaven from God, made ready as a bride adorned for her husband.* ³ *And I heard a great voice out of the throne saying, Behold, the tabernacle of God is with men, and he shall dwell with them, and they shall be his peoples, and God himself shall be with them, and be their God:* ⁴ *and he shall wipe away every tear from their eyes; and death shall be no more; neither shall there be mourning, nor crying, nor pain, any more: the first things are passed away.* ⁵ *And he that sitteth on the throne said, Behold, I make all things new. And he saith, Write: for these words are faithful and true.* ⁶ *And he said unto me, They are come to pass. I am the Alpha and the Omega, the beginning and the end. I will give unto him that is a thirst of the fountain of the water of life freely.* ⁷ *He that overcometh shall inherit these things; and I will be his God, and he shall be my son.* ⁸ *But for the fearful, and unbelieving, and abominable, and murderers, and fornicators, and sorcerers, and idolaters, and all liars, their part shall be in the lake that burneth with fire and brimstone; which is the second death.*

He shall wipe away every tear
And death shall be no more

Happy endings

Good enough

He asserts
Murderers
Sorcerers
And fornicators
There's a word
Will be transported
Into lakes of fire

Oh my

Who created us with genitals
And appetites for flesh?

What love of the metaphysical
Meaning souls alive
Drives us to channelers
For good news from the dead?

Why do we need the revelation
Of deliverance?

When does God
Bless his creation
With all its contradictions
And constraints?

In the meantime
Yes please
Wipe away our tears
We have been born into hunger
And cold
We live with the terminations of our own
The loss of everyone we love
And almost love

You say death shall be no more
Have you set a date
For immortality?
Or does rebirth come again
After multiple lifetimes
In this valley of tears
And unforgettable splendor?

All of it
Black and white
Red and blue
Sweet and sour
The majesty of mud
Shit
Emeralds
Spring

We embrace it all
We stand our ground
The children of earth

We are the ones remaining

As you delivered us

THE GREATEST OF THESE

First Corinthians 13:1–13

¹ *If I speak with the tongues of men and of angels, but have not love, I am become sounding brass, or a clanging cymbal.* ² *And if I have the gift of prophecy, and know all mysteries and all knowledge; and if I have all faith, so as to remove mountains, but have not love, I am nothing.* ³ *And if I bestow all my goods to feed the poor, and if I give my body to be burned, but have not love, it profiteth me nothing.* ⁴ *Love suffereth long, and is kind; love envieth not; love vaunteth not itself, is not puffed up,* ⁵ *doth not behave itself unseemly, seeketh not its own, is not provoked, taketh not account of evil;* ⁶ *rejoiceth not in unrighteousness, but rejoiceth with the truth;* ⁷ *beareth all things, believeth all things, hopeth all things, endureth all things.* ⁸ *Love never faileth: but whether there be prophecies, they shall be done away; whether there be tongues, they shall cease; whether there beknowledge, it shall be done away.* ⁹ *For we know in part, and we prophesy in part;* ¹⁰ *but when that which is perfect is come, that which is in part shall be done away.* ¹¹ *When I was a child, I spake as a child, I felt as a child, I thought as a child: now that I am become a man, I have put away childish things.* ¹² *For now we see in a mirror, darkly; but then face to face: now I know in part; but then shall I know fully even as also I was fully known.* ¹³ *But now abideth faith, hope, love, these three; and the greatest of these is love.*

. . . but have not love
I am nothing

Do I have love
Amidst my incessant
Questioning?

Do I have love
In the middle of the night
Dreaming
Of the day to come
With its scheduled animosity
Over everything
From scrambled eggs
To two-faced friends?

Do I have love
For firestorms and tsunamis
Parking lot massacres
Fraudulent executives
War-mongering senators
All full steam ahead
Without a mother's touch?

How can I be kind
When I cry out
To good gods in the foothills
And mother immaculates

And hear nothing
in return?

Love never faileth
Go the written words
Except when it's unknown
And silent
And too terrified to speak

I say I have put away childish things
The truth is
I am still newborn

I embrace my teddy bear
And sleep with a maniacal terrier
Who dreams of chasing squirrels
and demolishing sanitation trucks

The wilderness is real enough
Love more terrible
Than it might seem

. . .*but have not love*

I am nothing. . .

Some say
Where there is nothing
There is God

In which case

We shall see

JESUS

Matthew 11:25–30

25 *At that season Jesus answered and said, I thank thee, O Father, Lord of heaven and earth, that thou didst hide these things from the wise and understanding, and didst reveal them unto babes:* 26 *yea, Father, for so it was well-pleasing in thy sight.* 27 *All things have been delivered unto me of my Father: and no one knoweth the Son, save the Father; neither doth any know the Father, save the Son, and he to whomsoever the Son willeth to reveal him.* 28 *Come unto me, all ye that labor and are heavy laden, and I will give you rest.* 29 *Take my yoke upon you, and learn of me; for I am meek and lowly in heart: and ye shall find rest unto your souls.* 30 *For my yoke is easy, and my burden is light.*

Come unto me, all ye that labour and are heavy laden, and I will give you rest

Away in a manger
In the middle of nowhere
Comes
The Second Person of the Blessed Trinity

Is that so?

A portal to universal love
That's one way of putting it
Jesus the perfect metaphor
More probably an entrance
To the terrors of the mind

Layers of knowing and unknowing
Questions without answers
Pointing us
To the blindness beyond the light

Jesus the Jew
Telling us man is the incarnation of God
The physicalization of what otherwise
We would not know

Is that so?

Without Jerusalem
And its centuries of questioning
Confronting the unknowable
Scribbling wisdom
Would we still be worshipping the sun?

And ourselves?

Jesus crucified until the end of time
Says St. Paul
Saul
Whoever you are
Another portal into horror
Blatherin'
As if we did not already know
G-d is not easily come by

Protestants
Please take note
Don't care much for hanging flesh
Emphasizing rather the Divine
Or so they say

What you do unto the least of these

Said the carpenter

You do unto me

Staking his territory of the heart

For our evangelicals
A question:
Whatever happened to the Prince of Peace?
Is your Lord and Savior
Another face of Thor?
Onward Christian Soldiers says it all
A Mighty Fortress is our God
Jesus behind the barricades

Questioning remains the better metaphor
The better proof
Exploring gods beyond gods
Truth beyond truth
Adonai Adonai

Come unto me, all ye that labour and are heavy laden, and I
will give you rest

God revealed in the flesh
And bones
Of a rabbi from Nazareth

Is that so?

THE END

Do we once again
Worship
An anthropological deity
This time around
Called Jesus Christ?

Is that why he incarnated
Wearing a theological term
We've been told is accurate?

Should we bow down before him
Expecting miracles?

Did we not know Spirit too
Before he came?
Did we not celebrate
The Parthenon
The Elgin marbles
Socrates
Aeschylus
Euripides
Antigone
The great pyramids
The Sphinx

The unrelenting splendor of the sky?

Not to mention
Goldenrod

Chicory
Licorice

Gershwin
Billie Holliday
And razzmatazz

Let's bring it down

How much cash
Do storefront fundamentalists
Televangelists
Not to mention the Vatican
Require?

They tell us
He died for our sins
Whatever that means

He is love
Compassion
Forgiveness
Sacrifice
Despite himself

Is that not adequate?

Hard work by all accounts

The end and the beginning

Where does it begin?

Where does resurrection end?

Jesus

The story of the sacred heart

About the Author

Tony Scully is a graduate of Boston College and the Yale School of Drama. Several of his plays have been produced on and off Broadway. He is married to veteran Broadway actor Joy Claussen. At Yale, he was a deacon at Battell Chapel under the Rev. William Sloane Coffin Jr.

For five years afterwards, Scully was Project Director of the Jesuit-sponsored Woodstock Center for Religion and Worship at the Interchurch Center, 475 Riverside Drive, New York. Its mission: the exploration and renewal of liturgy in collaboration with leading anthropologists, sociologists, psychologists, and theologians. During that time, he also wrote a series of Prayers of the Faithful for Benziger Brothers, a liturgical press.

In his earlier career, for fourteen years Scully was a Jesuit in the Maryland Province of the Society of Jesus. During the seventies, Woodstock College, the Province school of theology, was affiliated with Union Theological Seminary in New York City.

In Los Angeles, in addition to writing for the entertainment industry, Scully directed The Return to Innocence Foundation, established by Garrett O'Connor MD and Fionnula Flanagan to deal with the multi-generational effects of cultural abuse in target populations. After moving to Camden, South Carolina from Los Angeles in 2005, Tony Scully was elected Mayor of the city.

He continues to write, direct, and serve as a theater and writing coach; he serves on boards of the region's arts and historical organizations.

Tony Scully is the author of *A Carolina Psalter* (Wipf & Stock, 2019).

9 781725 279971